PEW
PROMPTERS

A  DRAMA RESOURCE

PEW
PROMPTERS

The Complete Book of Short Sketches for
Sermons, Services, and Special Seasons

by Lawrence G. Enscoe
& Andrea J. Enscoe

 PUBLISHING COMPANY

KANSAS CITY, MO 64141

Questions? Please write or call:
    Lillenas Publishing Company
    Drama Resources
    P.O. Box 419527
    Kansas City, MO 64141
    Phone: 816-931-1900 ● Fax: 816-412-8390
    E-mail: drama@lillenas.com
    Web site: www.lillenas.com/drama

Cover art by Crandall Vail
Illustrations: Keith Alexander

Dedicated . . .

This collection is dedicated
to the Rev. Jack Chisholm.

And to his strong heart
for Jesus.

Contents

Preface

Drama.

It's finally happening.

As never before, churches and Christian groups across the country and around the world are now sharing the pulpit with the ministry of drama. Churches are using short sketches and monologues on a weekly basis—and other groups have seen the palpable results of using live drama at the core of their outreach.

Those of us who have been working with this powerful gospel tool in the last several decades are chorusing our "amens"—and breathing sighs of relief. We always firmly believed the church would discover the startling strength of drama. And that it would be an indispensable vehicle to reach TV-taught generations that learned the values of the world at the foot of the set. We believed congregations would respond with enthusiasm to the familiar medium—only now offering living, breathing images of God's power and the messages He has for those with ears to hear.

And they are hearing. And seeing.

And why not? If Jesus could tell dramatic stories with interesting characters and dialogue, why can't we? From the beginning of time, humankind has loved to hear a good story. And we Christians have plenty of those—tough, painful, ennobling, nurturing, life-changing stories about the love and passion of God for His people.

That's just what *Pew Prompters* is all about. Short, small-cast, easy-to-stage sketches and monologues for all ages based on what we experience as Christians in the church. There are humorous and thought-prompting dramas on baptism, Communion, church cliques, evangelism, missions, gossip, tithing, and Christian community.

Also included is a series designed to outfit a pastor or worship leader with dramas for the entire church calendar—Christmas, New Year's, Palm Sunday, Good Friday, Easter, the Fourth of July, Mother's Day, Father's Day, and Thanksgiving.

Don't just sit there. Call up a few people. Agree on a rehearsal time (Tuesday morning at 5 A.M.?), and start acting on the power and blessings of God.

We look forward to hearing and seeing what happens. God bless your time, talent, and labor.

Lawrence and Annie Enscoe
October 1990

PART ONE:
SKETCHES ON CHURCH LIFE

Are We Talking Gross or Net?

A Sketch on Tithing
Loosely Based on Acts 5:1-11

Cast

S.: a woman of whatever age
A.: her husband, a man of whatever age

Scene

S. and A.'s kitchen

Props

Kitchen table
Chairs
Papers
Ledgers
Checkbooks

Bank statements
2 calculators
Chalkboard
Dictionary

Costumes

Modern

Running Time

6-7 minutes

Production Notes

Comedy likes to go over the top—allow itself to become outrageous—in order to pay off a joke and make clear a message. That's certainly the case with this sketch. We took the idea of a couple trying to get out of tithing to the nth degree of lunacy. In the end, we hope we've made the point that tithing is non-negotiable. God is not the IRS. He only audits you once.

This is a farce, so let the energy build at each new discovery. Timing is very important, as A. is firing out data and S. is busy figuring away on her calculator. Don't be afraid to go over the top. The scene certainly gives you room to do it.

(Lights. A kitchen. A table smothered in papers, ledgers, checkbooks, and bank statements. A large, freestanding chalkboard. S. is standing at the chalkboard. A. is sitting at the table, ledger open and pencil in hand. S. writes a huge 10 on the board. Beat. She writes a percent sign.)

S.: 10 percent. That's the magic number.

A.: That's the . . . nut.

S.: That's right. That's the nut. 10 percent of our income.

A.: To go to the church?

S.: That's right. 10 percent to go to the church.

A.: Can't we pay it in installments or something?

S.: That's what we were supposed to do! It's called the offering plate, remember? But *you* kept forgetting your checkbook.

A.: Every Sunday?

S.: *Every* Sunday. For the whole year. And now we have to catch up. 10 percent. Right off the top.

(A beat.)

A.: Are we talking net or gross?

S.: What?

A.: Is that net or gross? 10 percent of our net or gross income.

S.: I don't know. I think it's gross.

A.: Come on! Not net? You can't mean 10 percent of the gross!

S.: Yes, I'm sure it's gross. I know it's gross. *(A beat.)* What's the difference between gross and net?

A.: Look, gross is . . . ah, net is when you . . . I forget. I always forget the difference. It's like sit or set, you know. I always forget that one. Does a chair sit or set?

(S. *leaves the room.*)

Or like further and farther. I always get confused. Do you say, "It's a mile further," or, "It's a mile farther"? Or like . . . like . . . in or into. Do you . . . like put your hand *in* fish guts or *into* fish guts—?

S. (*comes in reading a dictionary*): That's gross.

A.: What is?

S.: It's 10 percent of gross! Okay? Net is what you have after taxes. We're supposed to give up 10 percent of our gross.

A.: Now that *is* gross! 10 percent of everything we bring home? He couldn't mean that. (*A beat.*) Hey, wait a minute. Isn't there something in the New Testament about a net?

S.: That only applies if you're in the fishing trade. You had to go and become a florist.

A.: All right. Let's get on with this, can we? (*Works on the calculator.*) Okay, 10 percent of my . . . gross income is . . . (*Mouth drops open.*)

S. (*also working on the calculator*): 10 percent of what I bring home is . . . (*Mouth drops open.*)

(*They stare at each other.*)

A.: This is ridiculous!

S.: What does God need with all this? Doesn't He want us to be able to pay *our* bills?

A.: Bankruptcy can't be part of His divine plan.

S.: It's in Chapter Eleven.

A.: We've gotta figure something else out. Maybe I could just take all the tithe money down to the church and start throwing it up in the air.

S.: What?

A.: I figure, whatever God wants, He'll take.

S.: This is serious. (*Goes to the chalkboard and erases it.*) I've got a better idea. Let's do some massaging here.

A.: Honey, the kids are in the next room.

S.: No! Massaging the figures!

A.: Oh.

(S. *writes TIME = MONEY on the board.*)

S.: Time equals money, doesn't it? Why should it be any different for church? What we need are some deductions. Work with me here.

A.: I'm with you! Okay, okay. All right. *(Thinks.)* Hey, weren't we both in the Christmas cantata this year?

S. *(figuring on the calculator)*: That's right. Okay, okay. That's three hours every Thursday night for two months, plus two performances. I'll figure this by what you and I make an hour.

A.: And we offered to pick up the donated pine trees!

S.: That's mileage *and* wear and tear. Good. *(Figures.)* You're kidding! Wow. Let's do that again next Christmas. Incredible deduction. What else can you think of?

A.: We were at . . . six "spruce-the-church" Saturdays. *And* we brought our *own* tools.

S.: Okay . . . that's about four hours each day . . . wear and tear. Ew, that's a good one.

A. *(excited)*: Okay. Get ready. There's setting up the all-church banquet . . . I substituted in the Sunday School about eight times . . . we drove the youth group to Rageoid Mountain Splashdown last summer . . . I donated altar flowers about 20 Sundays . . . we worked in the church soup kitchen a couple'a times . . . there was the all-church meeting in January . . . I played a disciple in the Easter Last Supper Tableaux . . . that's rehearsals, performances, and wear and tear on your bathrobe . . . and we took Pastor Johannson out to dinner!

(S., *who has been figuring furiously, suddenly looks up.*)

S.: What about doughnuts?

A.: Huh?

S.: We brought doughnuts to Sunday School a couple of times.

A.: Yeah! Doughnuts. Oh . . . oh, here's a big one . . . I can't believe I didn't remember this one right off. Usher.

S.: That's right! Give it to me!

A.: I ushered . . . probably 45 Sundays. That's an hour every Sunday!

S.: Come on, Pastor never finishes the sermon on time.

A.: Okay, *two* hours!

S.: That's more like it.

A.: The family soup suppers and Bible studies. There's mileage driving the kids to VBS and back. Sunday clothes—that includes dry cleaning, shoe polish, Tide. What about the time we spent witnessing to the neighborhood and inviting them to church? That's publicity work.

S.: Okay. How much time do you figure we spent doing that?

(A beat.)

A.: Okay, forget that one.

S.: We're so close! Give me a couple more. Come on, think!

A.: Okay, okay . . . we bought pancake breakfast tickets. Donated clothes to the Salvation Army. Then there's the breakfasts at Dennys after church.

S.: What?

A.: We talked about the service, didn't we? It was a meeting!

S.: You're right. Okay, one more.

A.: Okay . . . I . . . I . . . I got it! I got it! Family devotions at home! Prayer time and Bible reading at the dinner table! Saying prayers with the kids at bedtime!

S.: Talk to me! Talk to me!

A.: That makes this place . . . A HOUSE OF GOD!!

S.: Yes, yes!

A.: Deduct the mortgage! Gas and electric!

S. *(wildly punching the calculator buttons)*: That's it! That's what we needed! Hold on . . . stand back . . . We owe the church . . . *(a final button)* . . . NOTHING!!

A.: What?!

S.: We don't owe them a dime in tithes! Nada! Zippo! In fact . . . hold on . . . *(figures quickly)* . . . THEY OWE US THREE HUNDRED AND TWENTY-FIVE DOLLARS!

A.: I'll call the pastor right now!

S.: Wait a minute. Hold on. We've got one more bit of business we have to take care of.

A.: What now?

S.: The building project.

A.: The what?

S.: Don't you remember? The pastor talked about the new Sunday School building the church needed. You were so moved by his words you told him when we sold the family property up in Shinola you'd donate all of it. Well, we sold it a month ago.

A.: I SAID WHAT?! Why didn't you kill me before I could speak!

S.: I tried to tell you to shut up. You wouldn't listen.

A.: *All* of it? I must have been out of my mind! Okay, okay. Let's think about this for a moment. *(A beat.)* How about if we just give 'em half.

(Blackout.)

A Hefty Donation

A Sketch on Mission Support

Cast

BEATRICE: a woman in her 30s
BART: her husband, a man in his 30s

Scene

A front room

Props

4 Hefty bags

Costumes

Modern

Running Time

3 minutes

Production Notes

"A Hefty Donation" is a humorous (and sad) look at the way we sometimes treat the church's missionaries when the time comes to give to their ministry.

God always expects us to give what is right, not what's left.

If you're adventurous, you can actually go out and find some of the items mentioned in the sketch and pull them out of the Hefty bags. Maybe you still have some in your closets.

(*Lights.* BART *and* BEATRICE *come in with two huge, bulging Hefty bags apiece. They set their loads down with a great sigh.*)

BART: Incredible. We have so much junk around here, I'm embarrassed. We really should go through things around here on a more regular basis. We need to simplify our lives. Extricate ourselves from the entanglement of possessions. Pare down our material world to a decent size, you know what I mean?

BEATRICE: Or get a storage unit.

BART: Hey, there's an idea.

BEATRICE: What did you get out of the cupboards?

BART: It's incredible the stuff we had back there. 14 cans of prunes. Did you know we had 14 cans of prunes?

BEATRICE: That's because my mother stayed with us last year.

BART: Oh, yeah. There was a can of grits. I have no idea who bought that. Ewww, some sardines and pimentos?

BEATRICE: From when I was pregnant.

BART: Oh, yeah. Old packages of diet food from that weight loss program you were on. There must have been a whole shelf of that stuff. Did you ever eat *any* of it?

BEATRICE: I found I could follow the diet better by mixing and matching alternative foods of my own choice.

BART: Did it work?

BEATRICE: What's that supposed to mean?

BART: Ah, there were cans of stuff with the labels so faded I had no idea what they are. Could be cream corn or water chestnuts, who knows? Hey, who bought 13 cans of vegetarian burger mix?

(BEATRICE *looks at him.*)

Oh, that one didn't work, either, huh?

BEATRICE: Change subjects. You want to know what I got?

BART: Sure.

BEATRICE: I got two bags of clothes from the 1970s. The 1970s, Bart. Waffle stompers, bell-bottom cords, angel flight pants, Ditto jeans, ribbed, pullover sweaters, shoes with heels four inches high, white belts six inches wide. I found clothes that haven't fit either of us since Carter was in office. I found a pair of overalls with holes in them that would get you arrested if you wore 'em.

BART (*grabbing the bag*): My *overalls?!*

BEATRICE: Touch them and die.

BART (*pulling his hand back, pouting*): Well, we could patch 'em.

BEATRICE: Bart, I found a shirt with Boy Scout achievement badges sewn all over it! I found a Gunne Sax dress! I found chokers, mood rings, and shirts with collars wider than Orson Welles! What are we still doing with all this stuff!

BART: We could keep it all until it comes back in fashion.

BEATRICE: Bart, if this stuff comes back into fashion I'm moving to Tibet.

BART: Well, we're getting rid of it, that's what we're doing. So, what do you say, Bea, we take all this junk down to the Salvation Army right now, huh? Let's load it all up and drive it down right now.

BEATRICE: I can't, Bart. I'd be too embarrassed to drop this stuff off to anyone. Honey, nobody in their right mind would be caught dead wearing this stuff in public. Not even someone with tape on his glasses and a pocket protector would wear clothes like this. And no one would eat a whole shelf of diet food if they didn't already pay big money for it! Come on, let's take all this garbage down to the dumps.

BART: Wait a minute! I have a better idea. (*Smiles.*) Oh, you're gonna love this!

BEATRICE: We build a bonfire in the backyard?

BART: No, we take it down to church! Are you with me?

BEATRICE: Yeah, yeah—

BART: Then we can—

BART/BEATRICE: GIVE IT TO THE MISSIONARIES!!!

BEATRICE: It's the least we can do.

(*Blackout.*)

The More Things Change

A Monologue on the Changing Church

Cast

ELDERLY PERSON: a man or a woman in his or her 70s

Setting

A church sanctuary

Props

Chair
Hymnal

Costume

Modern

Running Time

6 minutes

Program Notes

"The more things change, the more He stays the same." Truer words were never spoken. But the simple and difficult fact is: things do change. And so each generation finds new ways to express the power of Jesus and new ways of understanding Him. This sometimes causes conflict with the generation that has come before and is used to a particular expression of worship. It is up to all believers to find the sensitivity of the moment and the perception of the eternal.

Don't rush the monologue. If the role will be played by a younger person, take the time to move slowly and with purpose. When pauses are indicated, they mean the actor is thinking the thoughts that lead to the next words and ideas. Let your audience see the brain clicking.

The musical cues can be live or on tape. Tape is preferable to the spirit of this piece.

(In the darkness, an organ plays "Nothing but the Blood." Lights. A church sanctuary. An ELDERLY PERSON *is standing and singing with eyes closed. The hymnbook in his or her hands is closed.)*

ELDERLY PERSON: This is all my hope and peace—
            Nothing but the blood of Jesus.
            This is all my righteousness—
            Nothing but the blood of Jesus.

            Oh, precious is the flow
            That makes me white as snow.
            No other fount I know,
            Nothing but the blood of Jesus.

(The hymn ends. ELDERLY PERSON *looks around, nods, and sits with a sigh. Pause.)*

Now they always put the words of the hymns up on that whatziwhozit. That projector thing. *(Points.)* Up there. Don't even know why we need hymnals anymore. Words are all up there. Can you see? And most folks can't read music anymore. Stopped teachin' it in school a while back, didn't they? *(Holds up the hymnal.)* So what's the point'a these anymore, huh?

(Pause.)

Ah, I don't need that projector gizmo, anyway. *(Taps forehead.)* I've got all that beautiful music right up here.

(Closes eyes and sings.)

    Day by day, and with each passing moment,
    Strength I find to meet my trials here.
    Trusting in my Father's wise bestowment,
    I've no cause for worry or for fear.
    He whose heart is kind beyond all measure
    Gives unto each day what He deems best,
    Lovingly its part of pain and pleasure,
    Mingling toil with peace and rest.

(Long pause. It almost looks like ELDERLY PERSON *has forgotten where he or she is. Then the eyes come open and* ELDERLY PERSON *smiles.)*

I'm sorry. That song's always meant a lot to me. Some of these choruses we sing now, they sound like they were written for a . . . TV commercial or

21

something. No grace. No elegance. Nothin' to think about in the words. Ah.

(Pause.)

Last week they used one of those videeyos in the service. Took the lights down like it was a movie house or something and down comes the screen. I was lookin' for the Porky Pig cartoon. Why can't they just tell a story anymore. Use their brains and their mouths. That's what Jesus did. He didn't have no . . . videeyo thingamajig. I just wonder what it's going to be like in 20 years around here. We all going down to the Bijou to watch a church service? Not that I'm going to be around to see it.

(Pause. Looks around.)

It's all changed around here. Everything. I look around, and I hardly recognize things. I could be on Saturn or Venus sometimes. It's all changed so much. The way people dress to come to church anymore. The haircuts. The lack of haircuts. Scribblin' sermon notes in those . . . Day Runner calendar things everyone seems to carry around these days. I just don't know.

(A piano begins to play, softly.)

Oh. *(Standing.)* They're singing one of those choruses I was telling you about. Every Sunday, the same. *(Stops. Looks around at the faces.)* Sure must mean somethin' to 'em. I don't understand it. They . . . look at 'em. They sure love Jesus, though. You can see that. Just look around. It's written all over their faces. *(Smiles.)* Over there. That's Susan Johnson. Clyde Hannersol's daughter. She's a city commissioner. My poppa would have flipped over that! She's a dear, sweet believer, I can tell you that. The godliest woman. Calls me every week just to make sure I'm okay. Lost her husband two years ago. Cancer.

(Shakes head. The piano stops. Elderly Person *sits. Small pause.)*

My poppa. He was a tough old bird. The kind of man who'd frown when they read the Scriptures about love and forgiveness. He liked Proverbs on work, against sloth. His favorite Gospel story was Jesus cursin' the fruitless fig tree. They'd tell that story and you could see a little smile right there. Just the hint of one. I liked to see him smile.

(Pause.)

Oh, he was furious when they started doin' services here in English instead of the Old Language. When they brought a piano in here—whooo! "What is this, a dance hall?" 20 years ago a young gal sang a hymn on a guitar right up there. Poppa stormed out. Didn't come back to church for two months. Shook his boat too much. Maybe if she'd sung it in the Old Language . . . ?

(Pause. Smiles again.)

That's Harlan Jacobson over there. He does all the videeyo stuff around here. Nice kid. He goes around to the schools with some film he made and talks about stayin' away from drinkin' and what all kids are into. I just wish we'd've had someone doin' that 30 years ago. Seems to me we waited too long. Maybe my daughter wouldn't have . . . well . . .

(Takes a breath. Small pause.)

I remember when my daughter came out for a visit. Couple a months ago, maybe. I started in tellin' her all the things I've been tellin' you. How things have changed around here. She looks at me and says, "You know, sometimes things have to change to stay the same." Ah. Sounded like somethin' you'd get out of a fortune cookie. But I've thought a lot about that since. I've been thinkin' . . . maybe each generation has to discover the power of Jesus in their own way, you see. Their own way.

(Sighs. Small pause.)

People have changed. There's no two ways about it. They're different now. I wonder. I wonder if you can stay the same after what I've seen in the last 76 years. What we've all seen. *(Laughs.)* I mean, if Saint Peter walked into my poppa's church, the old fisherman probably would have had a stroke! But, Ol' Peter would have heard the name of Jesus bein' lifted up, I can tell you that. Just like He is right here. Then Ol' Peter'd take a deep breath. He'd sit back, close his eyes, and smile. There's somethin' that never changes, he'd say. There's somethin' to hold on to.

(The organ begins playing "His Name Is Wonderful." ELDERLY PERSON *sits back, eyes closed and smiling. The lights fade to:*

(Blackout.)

You First

A Sketch on Visitation Ministry/Evangelism

Cast

JENNIFER STEINER: a woman in her 20s to 40s
JIM STEINER: her husband, also in his 20s to 40s

Scene

A front porch

Costumes

Modern

Props

Door frame
Potted plants
2 Bibles
2 Day Runners

Running Time

6 minutes

Production Notes

"You First" is more than just a comic look at a husband and wife's difference of opinion, it's an outrageous look at two very different ministry styles. In presenting the gospel, one of them believes it's the heart of Jesus that counts, the other has more of a heart for head counts.

This scene can be played with just a door frame and some potted plants to outline a porch.

Jim and Jennifer Steiner can be in their 20s to 40s. If you decide to play beyond those ages, the dialogue will probably need some minor adjustments.

One caution in the playing. Both characters are angry. Make their fight feel real. It's better if Jim isn't the raging, outrageous fool and Jennifer the sweet, coolheaded spouse. That looks too much like preaching. So disguise the message in reality.

(Lights. A doorstep. A door frame, perhaps. A doorbell in the frame. Potted plants to outline the porch. JIM *and* JENNIFER *enter, each carrying a Bible and a Day Runner. It's obvious they are livid with each other. They stop at the door.)*

JIM: You first.

JEN: You know I don't like to go first. I do better once we get inside. I don't like to do the greeting and icebreaking stuff. Makes me too nervous.

JIM: Too bad. I knocked first at the other place, now it's your turn. *(A beat.)* Jen, would you knock.

JEN: Are you sure we have the right house?

JIM *(sighs and opens his Day Runner):* Richard and Linda Yale, 1125 Erie Street. This is the place, Jen. Knock.

JEN: Maybe I should ring the bell.

JIM: Always have an opinion, don't you.

JEN: I'm just telling you what I think.

JIM: This is ministry, Jen. You're not supposed to think. You're supposed to do. Now knock.

JEN: I just think the bell is . . . kinder, gentler.

JIM: You running for the presidency or what? We're not here to be gentle, Jen. We're here to shake these people up. Shake up their spiritual lives! The church doesn't send us out on visitation ministry to baby these people!

JEN: Jim, these people are first-time visitors who asked for the ministry team to come to their home. You have no idea if their spiritual lives need shaking up.

JIM: They said they were visitors, right? Which means they're not attending church, right? So what does that tell you about 'em?

JEN: You've already figured out what they need before we've even rung the bell. What if they just moved into the area. Maybe they just became Christians. You have no idea.

JIM: And we won't unless you knock.

JEN: I said I'm going to ring the bell.

JIM: Oh, that's just like you! Ring the little bell. Play a little bit of Muzak. Make everyone feel all warm and fuzzy. Don't upset the apple cart. Don't ask uncomfortable questions. Just say nice little things like, "Oh, I'm sorry that happened to you," and "I can understand how you could feel that way."

JEN: And it's just like you to pound on the door and let the whole world know Jim Steiner is here to straighten everything and everybody out.

JIM: Look, we only have a very short time to figure out where these people are at. We have to determine what they want as quickly as possible. What are they looking for in a church. What will they settle for, and what can they do without. And how much are they willing to spend. Then we need to fill them in on what we have to offer. What kind of guarantees they get with this particular package. Then you hook 'em. You don't baby 'em. You ask the hard question. You close the sale. "Are you in or out?" "Do we have a deal or don't we?"

JEN: It's no surprise you became a car salesman.

JIM: That's right! I'm pitching the gospel, that's what I'm doing. And don't forget it! I don't have time for small talk. Chitchat about kids and jobs and personal heartaches. Nossir! We might have this *one* opportunity and that's all. So I watch for the signs. The body language. How fast they answer. How slow. Then I drop the Big One: "So, will we see you at church next Sunday, then, Mr. and Mrs. Schnagel?" That's the final pitch. Then I listen. If they speak first, I know we've got 'em.

JEN: I should never have let you sell Amway.

JIM: Knock, will you! We're wasting time!

JEN: Afraid they're going to go to another dealer?

JIM: I knew you weren't cut out for the visitation ministry. You're too soft. Too understanding. These people run rings around you with their sob stories. Well, sob stories do not a church pew fill!

JEN: Wow, can I write that one down? *Guideposts* magazine would pay big money for that little gem.

JIM: That's it. I'm just gonna have to tell the pastor you can't cut it. You can't produce the numbers. I'll probably have to team up with Walt Coverdale.

JEN: An insurance salesman. Now why doesn't that surprise me?

JIM: Walt Coverdale single-handedly filled the sixth pew at eleven o'clock all by himself!

JEN: Look, pal, I'm your wife, remember? You're stuck with me as a partner. So just back off.

JIM: I am not going in there with you. You . . . you cramp my style.

JEN: I *what?*

JIM: You throw me off! Look, that last home visit with . . . *(flips open his Day Runner)* . . . Mrs. Lieberman. She tells you she can't come to church every Sunday because she doesn't have a car, and *you* go and offer to drive her!

JEN: Yeah?

JIM: You get too involved! Mrs. Lieberman just didn't want to come to church bad enough. You made it too easy for her. Now we have to leave 10 minutes early every Sunday to pick her up for heaven knows *how* long!

JEN: You are out of your mind.

JIM: And . . . last week . . . with those . . . *(looks at his Day Runner)* . . . Anderson people. The wife tells you she wasn't sure about coming to church because she'd felt forgotten by some other church when she was sick a few years back and now she was afraid to commit herself.

JEN: What did I say that was so bad?

JIM *(looking at his notes)*: You said . . . *(her words)* . . . "Oh, I understand, Mrs. Anderson. I'm sorry that happened to you, but churches are made up of human beings and we all fail. I know I do. But Jesus knew you were sick. You're committing yourself to Him, not the church."

JEN: What was wrong with that?

JIM: Wishy-washy! Namby-pamby! Wimpy-wompy!

JEN: So what should I have said?

JIM: "Tell it to the marines! We've all had trouble in our day! It's part'a life! Quit yer whining! Now, are we gonna see you in church this Sunday or not?"

JEN: I'm sure glad Lazarus' sisters ran into Jesus instead of you at their brother's funeral. *(His voice.)* "Yeah? Your brother's dead? Well, that's life. What d'you want me to do about it, huh? What I wanna know is: am I gonna see you in Temple this Saturday or not?"

JIM: There you go throwing Scripture around! Just like you do on all the visitations! "Let's check what the Bible says about that," and "Here's what the Bible says about that."

JEN: Excuse me, but I thought we were here to talk about Jesus—

JIM: Wrong! They can hear about Jesus all they want—*in church!* It's *our* ministry to get their backsides in a pew!

JEN: Well, I don't know about you, but I'm here to talk about Jesus. If they end up coming to church, then fine. (*Holds up her Bible.*) See this? This makes me an ambassador of Christ. Get it? This is not a brochure on what kind of church models we've got in the showroom. (*A beat.*) Let me see your calendar book.

JIM: What?

JEN: Let me see it.

(*He hands it to her, suspiciously. She flings it open, finds a page, and rips it out.*)

JIM: What are you—?!

JEN: Uh-huh! Just what I thought. It's a quota sheet. (*Reads.*) "Jim Steiner, 8 sales closed. Walt Coverdale, 20." You guys are keeping *track*?

JIM: All right! So Walt bagged 20. That's because he doesn't have to go out on visitation with a wimpy wife.

JEN: Well, neither do you. (*Tears the sheet in half and drops it.*) I'll be waiting in the car. Good luck, Mr. Sensitive. Now I know what you meant when you said you were working on commission. Silly me! I thought you meant the Great Commission! (*She goes out.*)

JIM (*calling after her*): Jen. Jennifer! Come on. I'll tone it down a little, okay? Look, I promise I won't say, "Are you in or out?" once, all right? Hey, I won't even say, "You won't find a better deal in town." Jenny? Honey? What if they ask me how they can have eternal life or something like that? That's *your* department! (*A beat.*) YOU BIG BABY! (*Looks around in his Day Runner.*) Maybe I have a tract on salvation or something in here. Nah. "Power of Positive . . . ," "As a Man Thinketh" . . . Nothin' about the gospel. (*Picks up the torn quota sheet.*) Coverdale, you're an animal. (*Crumples the papers.*) Ah! Who cares what Walt's doing! (*Takes a deep breath.*) I'm just gonna go in there, get the commitments, shake some hands, and get out. If they have any questions, I'll tell 'em they can call the main office—I mean, the church. (*Another breath.*) Okay, okay. Let's bring 'em in!

(*He reaches up to knock. He stops. He sighs. He reaches up to knock again. No go. Pause. He looks around. He rings the doorbell.*)

(*Blackout.*)

Whoever Wrote 1 Corinthians 13 Did Not Have a Little Sister Named Zanny

A Teen Sketch on Practicing What Is Preached

Cast

ROBIN: an teenage girl
ZANNY: a preteen or junior high girl

Scene

Robin's bedroom

Props

Chair
Bible
Stuffed animals
Jeans skirt

Costumes

Modern teen

Running Time

6 minutes

Production Notes

This sketch is a humorous look at what happens when a teenager decides to put a sermon on "Love is patient and kind" into action. It follows the belief that waiting to feel patience and kindness is not the way to the heart, but *acting* patient and kind might bring the desired attitude.

This is another play where the dialogue has to stay snappy because of the static nature of the sketch. Make sure Robin has a clearly defined and different voice from herself for the Zanny puppet. It can be very different or kind of similar to Zanny's real voice.

Change the slang to what's popular in your neck of it. Feel free to change "New Kids on the Block" to whomever is staring back at you from *Bop* magazine this week.

(Lights. A bedroom. ROBIN is sitting in a chair. Stuffed animals on her lap and all around. An open Bible at her feet.)

ROBIN: Look, I know you've probably heard this verse before. I'm sure. But the pastor used it in his sermon today, and I freaked. All I could think was, "I'm too sure." It's right here. 1 Corinthians 13:4. "Love is patient. Love is kind. Love is not envious." I mean, get real. This really flips my switch, I gotta tell ya. I'm all sayin' to myself, "Robin, this is *imposeeblay*." You know what I mean? And so Pastor tells us to try putting it into practice. Just for one day and see what happens. You know, use someone who pushes your buttons a lot. Now, I don't mean I can't love anyone or anything like that. And I'm not sayin' I'm not all patient and kind and all that, y'know? It's just that . . . well, I'll give it to ya straight. I got a little sister, see. Her name's Zanny. And I can tell ya this. Whoever wrote 1 Corinthians 13 did not have a little sister named Zanny.

(Looks up to heaven.)

What's the deal with this verse, huh? God's got a Son, but it is way obvious He does *not* have a little sister.

(Sighs. A beat.)

Okay, okay. I'm gonna have to try this thing out. I'm gonna have to practice. The thing is, see, if I practice bein' kind and patient and all with Zanny, she'll think I'm goin' soft on her. And then life as I know it will be over. So I got this idea. It's called "The Zanny and Robin Show."

(Picks up stuffed animals.)

This one's me. This one's Zanny. Good choice, huh. Okay, okay. Here goes.

ROBIN (ZANNY's *voice; whiny, irritating)*: Hey, Robin! Mark Johnson called.

ROBIN: When?! When'd he call?!

ROBIN (ZANNY's *voice*): Oh . . . uh . . . about . . . two weeks ago.

ROBIN *(under her breath):* "Love is patient . . . love is patient . . ." What did Mark say, O Little Sister of Mine?

ROBIN (ZANNY's *voice*): Oh . . . he just wanted to ask you out or somethin'.

ROBIN: WHAT?! HE NOTICED I WAS ON THE PLANET?!

ROBIN (ZANNY's *voice*): But I told him you already had a date with Myron Snively.
(ROBIN *gasps.*)
Well, you did! Yeah-huh! You did!

ROBIN *(under):* "Love is patient . . . love is patient . . ." Yes, you did tell the truth, Zanny. And I'm very proud of you. Did he say he'd call back?

ROBIN (ZANNY's *voice*): He said he'd call this week t'ask you out for ice cream.

ROBIN: You're kidding!

ROBIN (ZANNY's *voice*): I told him to forget it.
(ROBIN *gags.*)
I told him you said you were this, like, gi-huge-icly fat cow and you were on this, like, massive diet.

ROBIN: AGGGGHHHHHHH!! *(Her animal pounces on "ZANNY," works her over and drop-kicks her into the audience.)* Well. Let's try "Love is kind," shall we? *(She gets another "ZANNY" animal.)* Hey, Zanny Bananny, what's the deal? You look awfully sad. Did you flunk fingerpainting again?

ROBIN (ZANNY's *voice*): Oh, hi, Robin Bobbinhead. I feel so bad. I really do.

ROBIN: Why, Little Zanny?

ROBIN (ZANNY's *voice*): Well, I accidentally taped over your New Kids on the Block videos with The Disney Channel.

ROBIN: AGGGGGHHHHHH! *(Drop-kicks "ZANNY" into the audience.)* Well, that was a massive failure. All right. I've got one more try. Let's go with "Love does not envy." *(Another "ZANNY" animal.)* Hey, Zanny Fanny, why d'ya look so happy? You're grinning from ear to pierced-long-before-I-was-ever-allowed-to ear.

ROBIN (ZANNY's *voice*): Mom and Dad just told me some really cool news.

ROBIN: What is it, O Sister of Mine? They're not gonna ground you for giving yourself a haircut, are they?

ROBIN (ZANNY's *voice*): Uh-uh. They just told me I could have a '66 Mustang on my 16th birthday.

ROBIN (under): "Love does not envy . . . love does not envy . . ." Why'd they tell you that, you little . . . kid?

ROBIN (ZANNY's voice): They said they loved me very, very much, and that I should never be deprived of radical transportation if I really wanted it.

(ROBIN is snorting.)

And besides, they said they didn't want me buggin' 'em for the car keys every five minutes like you used to—

ROBIN: AGGGGGGHHHHHH! (Jumps on "ZANNY," bops her good, drop-kicks her.) You slime! I'm the one who wants a '66 Mustang! But noooo! You think I like askin' for the car keys every five minutes, you buck-toothed little—

(Remembers the audience. A deep breath.)

Look, I am not envious, okay. But why should she get a car when she's 16 and I have to call Myron Snively. (A beat.) Okay. A little envy. A tad bit. (Dumps the animals.) Look, this just isn't going to work. I'm like . . . addicted to wailing on her. What am I supposed to do? Zanny . . . just expects it from me.

(A knock.)

Zanny? (A beat.) Zanny? (A beat.) Look, answer me, you little geek!

ZANNY (the real one; offstage): Can I come in?

ROBIN: Stay out.

(ZANNY comes in. She's holding a jeans skirt behind her back.)

ZANNY: You know your radical new jeans skirt? The one Mom said fit too tight in the rear because you keep buying size 5/6 when you should be buying 7/8.

ROBIN (infinite patience): Yes, Zanny.

ZANNY (holds the skirt up): I just spilled Nestle's Quick on it.

(ROBIN stifles a scream. She picks up a stuffed animal and drop-kicks it. She turns back to ZANNY with a plastered smile.)

ROBIN: You wanna tell me what happened?

ZANNY (tumbles out): See, I was showin' Ginah what a radical skirt it was 'n how I wanted to get one just like it, only in the right size, and I had it out on the kitchen table and that's how it happened.

(ROBIN takes the skirt and looks at it. She takes a deep breath.)

ROBIN (points to a stain): This the only place?

ZANNY: Uh-huh!

ROBIN: Doesn't look too bad. Let's see if Mom knows how to get it out.

ZANNY: I'm really sorry! Honest! I know I'm a geek, but I was just *showin'* it to Ginah! Honest!

ROBIN: I know you didn't mean to do it, Zanny, okay. You never *mean* to do it. Look, we'll work on it.

(They start to head off.)

Ah . . . listen, Zanny. Mom and Dad ever say anything to you about a '66 Mustang?

(Blackout.)

The All-Talk Gossip Party Line

A Teen Sketch on Gossip

Cast

ANNOUNCER: offstage voice
BABE: a girl in her teens
BOHUNK: a guy in his teens

Scene

A living room

Props

2 chairs
2 phones
Offstage microphone

Costumes

Modern hip

Running Time

4 minutes

Production Notes

This sketch about gossip is based on one of those late-night 900-number commercials where a guy can talk to 14 beautiful women sitting all together on one couch.

The announcer can either be performed onstage or from an offstage mike. Make sure the actors playing Babe and Bohunk model the gelled-hair, all-smiles delivery of those disgusting TV commercials. You might have to stay up past David Letterman to see one. Don't do it on a school night.

(*Lights.* BABE *and* BOHUNK *are on the phone. They mime talking, animatedly.*)

ANNOUNCER (*off*): Hey, dudes and babes! Are you lonely? Are you bored with life? Are you tired of those long Saturday afternoons with only reruns of "Gilligan's Island" and watching your baby sister eat things off the floor to make your existence bearable? Pretty scary, huh? Well, join the hundreds, maybe millions of young people who are filling in all the dead time talking on the telephone!

BABE: You're kidding me!

BOHUNK: No way, dude!

ANNOUNCER (*off*): That's right! It's the all new All-Talk Gossip Party Line. Just call 1-900-4Gossip and you can spend your Saturday afternoons talking with other bored, TV-tired teens with nothing better to do than talk about other people!

BABE (*to audience*): Talk about friends at church.

BOHUNK (*to audience*): Or school.

BABE: Even people you barely know!

ANNOUNCER (*off*): Yes, everybody's fair game on the All-Talk Gossip Party Line. Let's listen in on this dudical babe as she reaps the Gossip Line benefits.

BABE: Well, it just wouldn't surprise me about her. I just wouldn't doubt it is all I'm saying. You know, with her past and everything. You didn't know about her past? Before she started coming to church. Well, I'm certainly not gonna dish any cheese on her. No way, Ashleigh. Are you doy or what? I said my lips are sealed, all right? You're just gonna have to use your imagination. Nope. Uh-uh. I'm not gonna say a—okay, you're warm. No, my lips are—getting warmer. Ashleigh, it'd be totally uncool if I told you about—HOT! VERY HOT! Okay, all right. But I did NOT tell you, got it? So, with a past like that, you can kinda get the idea about what's goin' on between her and you-know-who from youth group. Yeah, I know we need to pray for her, okay? Hey, while we're on the subject, here's some other people we could pray for!

ANNOUNCER (*off*): And who said gossip couldn't be spiritual? And remember, don't be afraid to be vague. Letting the other party do some of the work is half the fun of the All-Talk Gossip Party Line. Let's listen in on this big-time Bohunk as he shares what's on his heart.

BOHUNK: It was a raucous party, dude! Way thumpin', I'm tellin' you. Hey, you know who I saw there. No. Mark. Dude, Mark Honig from youth group. If you'd'a been there, Major Flake, you'd'a seen 'im. He was Mr. Waistoid, I'm tellin' you. No doubt. He asked me not to tell anybody cuz he was ashamed of himself, so don't tell too many people, okay. Dude, check it out, you-know-who was there. No. Cheryl. Dude, Cheryl Anson from the college-and-career group. Yeah, well we may'a talked is all. Whaddayou mean, "What else happened?" (Smiles.) Yeah, you're right about that. I am pretty killer. Well, you just let your imagination run wild, dude. You're gonna think what you want to, anyways.

ANNOUNCER (off): Oh, don't let the facts stop you on the All-Talk Gossip Line. Besides, tell enough people and it becomes the truth anyway! So, don't be in the dark anymore about what's going on outside your living room. Call the All-Talk Gossip Line today.

BABE/BOHUNK: Nuh-uh! That's what his second cousin's brother told me! No doubt!

ANNOUNCER (off): Start taking charge of your life—and everybody else's. Call the All-Talk Gossip Line today. 90 cents for the first three minutes, two bits off of someone's reputation for every minute afterward. So call 1-900-4GOSSIP today. That's 1-900-4GOSSIP. And remember, it's not the truth, it's just all talk on the All-Talk Gossip Party Line!

(Blackout.)

Anointed with Oil

A Teen Mime Sketch on Christian Community

Cast

COG
WHEEL
CONNIE VAYER
LAST ONE IN LINE
MACHINE PART
THE MACHINE
All teen roles of whatever gender

Scene

A youth group room

Props

None needed

Costumes

Modern hip

Running Time

5 minutes

Production Notes

"Anointed with Oil" is based on the age-old "Machine" pantomime exercise where a group of actors play different parts of a machine. In this case, we discover the machine won't operate unless everyone is doing his part—and not everyone can do his part without a little help from his friends.

And that's what the Body of Christ is all about.

The "Machine" is in motion throughout the scene. It works like an assembly line, with actors moving a "product" from one end of the line, through some mechanical processes, and then stacked at the other. Each of the actors should make a noise pertaining to his "job" in the structure. Connie Vayer's oilcan bit is based on the Tin Man scene from the *Wizard of Oz*. You might want to give that a look.

When the "Machine" talks, lines are blurted out over the noise of the gizmos.

(A line of actors are onstage performing "The Machine" pantomime acting exercise. Each plays a part of the machine—hissing, pinging, and whirring toward some productive end. Only, in this machine, there are some key parts missing. The Machine chugs on a few moments, though it's perfectly clear the work is hindered. The actors frown and look around, wondering what's happening. The noises become more and more discordant and halting. COG and WHEEL come in, moving stiffly and mechanical, like rusted tin men.)

MACHINE *(different voices)*: Hey, where you guys been! Nothing's gettin' done over here! We need you! *(Together.)* SNAP TO! FALL IN! LINE UP!

WHEEL *(waves)*: Hey, Cog! Looks like we're in hot water again.

COG: Looks like it, Wheel. I'm movin' a little slow today. You?

WHEEL: Waxed.

(They do limber-up exercises.)

COG: I need to spend more time workin' out. I'm wasted.

WHEEL: No doubt. My joints are all—

MACHINE *(together)*: COME ON! *(Different voices.)* You're holdin' up progress! We gotta move ahead! Time's wasting! Hurry up! *(Together.)* MOVE IT!

COG *(to the Machine)*: Lookit, we need to be in shape or we're not gonna get anywhere.

WHEEL: No doubt.

(COG and WHEEL produce oilcans and lubricate their joints. They shake the cans.)

WHEEL: What a geek! I didn't bring a whole lot of oil today. I think I've got just about enough for one lube left.

COG: Same here. Hey, you guys bring any extra oil in case we—

MACHINE *(together)*: NO! *(Different voices.)* Getting oil's your job! I've only got enough for me! I didn't bring any extra! I oil up at home! *(Together.)* NOW GET IN LINE!

(COG *and* WHEEL *shrug and get in line. The Machine chugs along in harmony. In mime, something is passed down the line, over wheels, cogs, and gizmos.* THE LAST ONE IN LINE *turns, like a pair of robotic arms; and drops the "product" on the floor, making the sound of a crash.* LAST ONE *repeats the business.*)

MACHINE (*different voices*): Hey, what's going on down there?! What's that noise? What's breakin' down? We're doin' our part down here!

LAST ONE IN LINE: I can't help it, bozos! Somebody's missin'!

COG: Check it out. Where's Connie? Connie Vayer. She's not in her place at the end. We can't finish anything without her.

(*As they speak,* CONNIE VAYER *walks in. She grinds forward like a toy running out of power, then stops. A little forward, then stops. Finally, she halts and tips forward.*)

WHEEL: There she is.

CONNIE (*weakly; stiff-jawed*): Heeelp meee.

(*The Machine stops chugging.*)

MACHINE (*different voices*): She looks terrible! What's her problem? A couple'a quarts low, looks like t'me. She should'a taken care'a herself at home! (*Together*) I DON'T HAVE ANYTHING FOR HER!

CONNIE: Heeeelp meeee.

COG: Wheel, we gotta help her, or nothin'll get done.

WHEEL: Both'a us don't have any extra. You know that. I just got what I need in case I start to lose steam.

COG: How about it, everybody? Let's all oil her up, and we can—

MACHINE (*together*): THERE'S ONLY ENOUGH FOR ME!

CONNIE: Oiilcaaaaan.

COG: How about it, Wheel?

WHEEL: I can't afford to break down. I won't be able to do my part.

COG: Neither will I, bone! Nobody will, don't you get it? Lookit, if you give her a little and I give her a little, we'll both pull this off. And we'll have enough for the both of us. Got it?

WHEEL (*thinks a moment*): Got it.

(*They step out. Immediately the Machine goes discordant.* COG *and* WHEEL *oil* CONNIE'S *joints. She stands, moves her limbs, walks around. Tries to talk.*)

WHEEL: What's she sayin'?

COG: I think she said, "My mouth." She wants us to oil her jaw.

39

WHEEL: You think we could just leave that part rusty?

COG (*smacking him*): Oil it!

(*They oil each side of her jaw.*)

CONNIE: Wow! Thanks! You sweet things, you! What a relief. Now I can just move anywhere I want! Incredible! I just can't believe you two would sacrifice some of your own oil!

WHEEL: Told ya we should'a left it rusty.

MACHINE (*together*): COME ON!

(*They all jump back into line. The Machine goes into harmony again. CONNIE is there to pick up the imaginary product and carry it to the table, where she stacks the "product" up. For a moment, we listen to the well-oiled machinery.*)

MACHINE (*different voices*): That's better! Now we're cookin' with gas! With oil! What a sound! Purring like a cat!

(*One of the Machine parts suddenly halts a little.*)

MACHINE PART: Hey . . . I just felt a little stiffness. In my elbows, I think. Can anybody spare a little oil? I ran out this morning.

(*Silence. COG and WHEEL look at each other.*)

MACHINE (*different voices*): I think so. Sure. I gotta little extra in my back pocket. Gotcha, dude! Fix ya right up! No worries around here!

MACHINE PART: Thanks.

(*COG and WHEEL look at each other and smile. The Machine continues to purr as we go to . . .*

(*Blackout.*)

First Service or Second?

A Sketch on Church Cliques

Cast

PAULA MILLER: a woman in her 30s or 40s
AL MILLER: her husband, also 30s or 40s
LINDA DUNCAN: a woman in her 30s
CAMERON KITTRIDGE: a man in his 20s

Scene

A banquet hall

Props

Tables
Table settings
Chairs
Name cards
Menus

Costumes

Modern

Running Time

8 minutes

Production Notes

We all have our own routines; our own ways of doing things. Some of us might go to the grocery store the same day every week, taking the same route to get there. And how often do we sit with the same people at coffee break?

Sometimes, church is no exception to the rule. We attend the same service, the same Sunday School, talk with the same people. Some of us have our familiar patterns down to a science.

"First Service or Second?" takes a seriocomic look at how we can attend the same church for years and never meet one another. How our well-heeled habits, cliques, and directions can limit our "assembling together" to something more like assembly-line fellowship. The same parts go by every Sunday.

This sketch takes place entirely at a table, so keep the energy high and the pace moving to keep things from feeling claustrophobic.

(In the darkness, the sound of people milling around. Faint music in the background. Familiar Christian instrumentals. Lights. Several round tables dressed in banquet style. AL *and* PAULA MILLER *come in, quickly checking the name cards on the tables.)*

PAULA *(loud whisper):* Al! We're over here! Do you recognize anyone at this table?

AL: I don't know any of these names. None of 'em.

PAULA: Great. Just great. We're going to spend the next three hours of a church banquet with people we don't know from Adam!

AL *(picking up a card):* Or Eve. Do these people even *go* to our church?

PAULA: I've got an idea. Grab your card. Quick! Let's switch with Chuck and Millie Hackle over at that table over there. Then *we* can sit with Pastor and Mrs. Johnson *and* the Rodenbergs. *(She starts to go.)* Hold on. Chuck and Millie just sat down. We waited too long.

AL: How do they rate, getting to sit at the pastor's table? We started attending the church six months before they did.

(Without their seeing, LINDA DUNCAN *comes in, looking for her name tag. She finds it and sits at the Millers' table.)*

PAULA: Look! The Heidelbrechts aren't here yet! We can switch with them and sit with the Van Wingerdens!

AL: Too late. The Heidelbrechts just walked in. *(A beat.)* Hey, how about if I just get rid of those other two stooges at our table! I'll switch them with the Van Wingerden's, and they can sit with us. They like us better than the Heidelbrechts, anyways.

PAULA: Perfect.

AL *(to* LINDA *as he grabs her card):* Excuse me. *(Starts to walk away. Stops. Smiles.)* Ah . . . hello. I'm Al Miller. This is my . . . Ah, Paula?

PAULA *(turns; wanly):* Oh, hello there.

LINDA: The Millers. Right. I recognize both of you from your picture in the church directory.

AL: No kidding.

LINDA: What are you doing with my name card?

AL: I . . . oh, I thought it was misspelled. *(Shows it to* LINDA.) Didn't they misspell Linda?

LINDA *(reading):* L-I-N-D-A. No, that's it.

AL: I could have sworn they . . . oh, well. Honey, this is . . . *(reads card)* . . . Linda Duncan. She goes to our church. Imagine that!

PAULA: I . . . don't think I recognize you. The church is so big, though. Nice to meet you.

LINDA: Nice to meet you both.

AL: Well. *(A beat.)* Do you want to sit down, honey?

PAULA: Well, sure. This *is* our table, isn't it?

AL *(looks at the name cards):* Sure enough. There's our names, right there.

PAULA: Wonderful.

(They laugh and sit. Pause. AL *takes a drink of water. Crunches the ice.)*

LINDA: So. You two been attending here long?

PAULA: About 10 years.

AL: Uh-huh.

LINDA: I just moved into the area about a month ago. Haven't settled in yet, really. Started looking for a church right away, though. This was the first one I tried, and I liked it so much, I stayed.

PAULA: Well, it's a good church.

AL: Uh-huh.

(CAMERON comes in, looking the tables over for his place. He looks a little nervous.)

AL *(to* PAULA, *under):* Since when did they start inviting the high school group to these things?

LINDA: Are you Cameron?

CAMERON: I sure am.

LINDA: You're over here with us.

CAMERON: Oh, great. *(Smiles and sits. Pause. He holds his name card against his chest.)* Cameron Kittridge. *(Makes a camera click noise.)* Arrested for being dangerously late to church functions. *(Looks at the others. No response. Turns his head to the right and makes another camera noise.)* Sentenced to sit with people who don't think he's the least bit funny.

LINDA *(laughs, holds out her hand):* I think you're funny. I'm Linda Duncan. This is Al and Paula Miller.

*(*CAMERON *shakes their hands.)*

AL/PAULA: Hi.

LINDA: So, how long have you been going here?

CAMERON: First time I've ever been here. I like the tablecloths, though. Nice china. Oh, you mean the *church!* About two years.

LINDA *(laughs):* I've only been attending here for about a month. Al and Paula have been here for 10 years.

CAMERON: Really.

AL/PAULA: Uh-huh.

CAMERON: I'd love to be at a church for 10 years. Get to know everybody. Like a family. I'll bet you two know just about everybody.

AL/PAULA: Uh-huh.

(Small pause.)

AL: Well. This looks like a pretty good menu, huh? Chicken cordon bleu. Rice. Salad. Same company catered last year's banquet. Last year we had turkey, I think.

(Pause.)

LINDA: You know, I have to say, I've never seen any of you at church before. I've been there every Sunday like clockwork. I don't understand it. Though Cameron, you do look a little familiar.

CAMERON: So do you.

PAULA *(to* LINDA*):* Well, are you a first or second?

LINDA: Excuse me?

PAULA: Which service do you go to. Nine or eleven o'clock?

LINDA: Oh, the second. Ah, eleven o'clock.

AL: Well, that explains it.

PAULA: We *always* go to nine.

LINDA: I see.

CAMERON: I go to the nine o'clock.

AL: Well, which door do you come in?

CAMERON: Which door?

AL: South side or west side?

CAMERON (figures a moment): Ah . . . well, I park by the . . . thing . . . the . . . oh, the door by the doughnuts. The west side.

AL: Well, that explains it.

PAULA: We always come in the south side. Always. Then we go down the west aisle to the third row from the front, six spaces in. We've been doing that for the last seven years.

CAMERON: I'm always late. I usually sit in the overflow room. Or in the back.

AL: Well, that explains it.

CAMERON: But you go out the west side, don't you? That's where the doughnuts and coffee are.

PAULA: No, we always go out the south side past the nursery. Then we go around the north side to Calvin Hall for Sunday School.

CAMERON: Which Sunday School?

AL: Van Vechten's class. "Parents with Dual Incomes and Teenaged Kids." On the east side.

CAMERON: Well, I probably wouldn't run into you there.

PAULA: I wouldn't think so.

AL: Well, that explains it.

LINDA: I go to the "Single but Still Hopeful" class. That's in Calvin Hall, isn't it?

PAULA: Agnes Vandersolo's class? That's on the south side. You probably come in the door by the parking lot with the little flower boxes of mums?

LINDA: You're right.

PAULA: We used to come in that door. Five or six years ago. But not anymore.

LINDA: I see.

AL: Well, that explains it.

CAMERON: But that's the door I go out of. After Sunday School. That's where I've seen you before, Linda.

LINDA: Right. I go out that way over to the sanctuary.

CAMERON: Well, I'll stop and say hi this Sunday.

LINDA: Good. Now all we have to do is figure out the right directions to run into the Millers here.

(CAMERON *and* LINDA *laugh. The* MILLERS *don't.*)

PAULA: Well, it's really very easy. We leave the house at 8:36 and arrive at the south side lot at 8:49. We pull into the first row of parking stalls by the west sidewalk and travel to the south sidewalk up to the south side door. Then it's down the west side aisle to our seats next to the Heidelbrechts and the Van Wingerdens, who are usually there a few minutes early because they don't have teenagers. After the service we always go out the south side past the nursery and around to the north side directly to Sunday School. Down the east hallway to Van Vechten's class. The kids then travel on to the lower south side for their "Too Live Jesus" class. After Sunday School we talk with the Hackles and the Rodenbergs for five minutes, then we go to the south hallway via the east hallway, meet up with the kids, and go out the south side door back to the parking lot, having made one large, time-saving circle back to our car. We're usually home by 11:26.

(*Small pause.*)

AL: Well, that explains it.

CAMERON (*handing* PAULA *a napkin*): You lost me. Would you mind drawing a map? (*A beat.*) Just kidding.

LINDA: You never go any other route?

PAULA: It gets us where we need to go.

LINDA: But you don't get a chance to meet new people that way. Give people a chance to get to know you.

PAULA: We know plenty of people. We have a small group at our house every week.

AL: That's right. The Heidelbrechts, Van Wingerdens, the Hackles, and the Rodenbergs.

(*Small pause.* CAMERON *and* LINDA *glance at each other.*)

CAMERON/LINDA: Well, that explains it.

(*Blackout.*)

Christian Diversity

A Commercial on Christian Denominations

Cast

GUEST
HOST
MAN
WOMAN
WOMAN TWO
PITCHMAN
OTHER PARTYGOERS
All men or women of whatever age

Scene

A front room

Costumes

Modern

Props

Drinking glasses or cups
Cassettes
Pamphlet

Running Time

4 minutes

Production Notes

This is not a sketch pushing ecumenism. And it's not meant to denigrate or extol any denominational stance. It's simply a couple of gentle jabs at the ties that can really put us in a bind. How denominational boundaries can be a little confusing and, at times, disheartening. Sometimes we have to be honest and say that, yes, it's not diversity. It's division.

The sketch is also just meant to be a humorous look at ourselves.

All the denominational names have been made up to protect the innocent.

"Christian Diversity" is meant to be performed in satiric commercial style. As noted elsewhere, the PITCHMAN can be the veritable essence of smarm.

(In the darkness we hear party chatter. Lights. A front room. People are standing around, holding glasses and talking. GUEST shakes HOST's hand.)

GUEST: Boy, this certainly is a wonderful fellowship you have here. Thanks for inviting me, neighbor.

HOST: My pleasure. You've been living next door to me for . . . 10 years? And I never even knew you were a Christian. If I'd have known that, I would have invited you over a long time ago.

GUEST: Oh, I understand. You can't be too careful these days.

HOST: So true, so true. *(A beat.)* So, neighbor, what are you, anyway?

GUEST: What am I?

HOST *(laughing):* You know! What church do you . . . ?

GUEST: Oh, you want to know what church I go to.

HOST *(points to his nose):* That's it. You know, your . . . denominational allegiance, as it were.

GUEST: I see. Well, neighbor, I'm a Neo-Non-Denom-Charismatic.

(All chatter stops. Everyone turns to the GUEST, who looks around, nervously.)

HOST *(trying to stay calm):* Did you say, "Neo-Non-Denom-Charismatic."

GUEST: I don't know. Did I?

WOMAN: We're all Quasi-Neo-Fundies here, buster!

GUEST *(to HOST):* You're a Quasi-Neo—?

MAN: That's *Mr.* Quasi-Neo-Fundamentalist to you, pal!

WOMAN: And proud of it!

48

(Shouts of "Yeah!" and "That's right!")

GUEST: I see . . . *(Looks at his watch.)* Wow! Would you look at this! It's almost time for the "Old-Time Religion Hour"! I never miss that. Not on your life. *(Backing away.)* Thanks so much for inviting me. No, no, please, let me find my own way out.

(The party freezes. Piano tremolo. The PITCHMAN bounds in.)

PITCHMAN: How many times have you been caught with denominational egg all over *your* face? How many times have you barely gotten out of that "occupied territory" with your doctrines in one piece? Oh, isn't it embarrassing? I know. I've been caught behind the lines several times myself. What do you do? Do you mumble something really heathen like, "Well . . . to each his own!" and beat feet for the door? Do you laugh and say, "You know, some of my best friends are—." Or do you simply stand there with that stupid grin on your face just praying for the Second Coming. Well, now you'll never have to feel left out of it again!

(He holds up a set of cassettes.)

Not with Nerdman's "10 Minutes to Christian Diversity!" Yes, folks, this cassette collection will keep you up on 1,000 of the latest denominations, nondenominations, break-offs, spin-offs, split-offs, breakups, throwbacks, and reformations. Why, here's a tape on Neo-Reformo-Pentecostalists, Contempo-Charismatics, Neo-American-Liturgo-Liberalists, and Pento-Anglo-Methodists. And, of course, these tapes contain some of those "old-time religions." Why, just look! Here's "Evangelical"! Yes, just pop these tapes in at home or in your car, and you'll be given correct pronunciations, root denominations, founders' names, catchphrases, buzzwords, favorite televangelists—why, there's even a section where each denomination tells you what's wrong with everyone else! Now, you, too, can turn that embarrassing moment:

(The party unfreezes.)

GUEST *(backing away):* Quasi-Neo-Fundies?! I'm sorry! I didn't know!

PITCHMAN: Into spiritual triumph!

GUEST: Quasi-Neo-Fundies! Hallelujah! I'm finally among the faithful! What a joy! You know these Neo-Reformo-Fundies? Somebody oughta tell those guys where they can get off!

MAN: Amen to that!

(The party surrounds the GUEST.)

WOMAN: Where *do* you find such spiritual friends?

HOST: I dunno. Just blessed, I guess.

WOMAN TWO: He's so informed!

(GUEST *looks at the audience, smiles and nods.*)

PITCHMAN: But wait! There's more!

PARTY: MORE?

PITCHMAN: That's right! If you order today, we'll also send you this free pamphlet. (*Produces a booklet.*) "How to Win That Christian Argument."

(*The party applauds.*)

Yes, now you'll never have to say something incredibly wimpy like, "Well, brother, I guess you were right." No way. Not with this baby. Now you can turn that righteous anger into victory! Look, some of the chapters include: "Knowing Enough Greek to Be Dangerous," "Making Ecclesiasticus Work for You," and my personal favorite, "Verses Out of Context—Your Key to Success."

(*The party gathers around the* PITCHMAN, *gawking at the goods.*)

Yes, sir! "The Handbook of Christian Diversity" tape series and the "How to Win That Christian Argument" pamphlet can be yours for the low price of only $39.99. Plus postage and handling. Remember, you can't find these in any store. They're only available through this amazing TV offer. The address is: Spewed Associations, 1442 Complacent Corners, Warmwater, IL 60609. And remember, it's not division.

PARTY: IT'S DIVERSITY!

(*Blackout.*)

Myrtle Fetschwanger Explains It All to You

A Sketch on Church Greeting Programs

Cast

MYRTLE FETSCHWANGER: a woman in her 40s to 60s
LORI: a young lady in her mid-20s
PASTOR DORCUS: a man of any age

Scene

A church foyer

Props

Small table
Guest book
Potted palm
Free-standing tract rack
Day Runner
Bible
Bulletins

Costumes

Modern

Running Time

6-7 minutes

Production Notes

"Myrtle Fetschwanger" is a gentle jab at the "get 'em in, sign 'em up" method of church growth. This scene might be used in ushers or greeters training about what not to do when new people visit the church.

It's also just a fun look at a kooky character.

The actor playing Myrtle needs to consider the scene a monologue and plow right through any of Lori's lines. Don't let the pacing sag by allowing lag time between the dialogue.

(In the darkness, the sound of people milling around. Lights. A church foyer. A small table with a guest book. A potted fake tree. A free-standing tract rack. MYRTLE FET-SCHWANGER *is hiding back near the tree. She watches church "members" walk past, smiles, and waves.* MYRTLE *is 60ish, gray-haired, and wears glasses, a severe dress, and flowered hat. She carries a Day Runner. Suddenly, she darts out, then halts. False alarm. She goes back into hiding.* LORI *enters. Early 20s, shy. She carries a Bible and a bulletin thick with inserts. She is making a beeline for the church door.)*

MYRTLE *(leaping out, pointing):* YOU!

LORI: M-Me . . . ?

MYRTLE: There you are, you sweet little thing!

*(*LORI *backpedals as* MYRTLE *bears down on her.)*

MYRTLE: You're new here, aren't you?

LORI: W-well, I—

MYRTLE: You're a first-timer, I just know you are! Know how I can tell? You didn't know the tune to that little chorus we do. We always do that one, you know. It sure . . . exposes the newcomers! *(Thrusts out a hand.)* Fet-schwanger here.

LORI: Excuse me?

MYRTLE *(pumping* LORI's *hand):* Fetschwanger. Myrtle Fetschwanger.

LORI *(under):* You're kidding.

MYRTLE: And you are?

LORI: My name's Lori.

MYRTLE: Oh, yes. Fine. Fine! So nice to meet you. *(Singing it.)* Weeelcooome!

LORI: Well, thank—

MYRTLE: So, what did you think of our little service, hmmm?

LORI: Oh. Well, I thought it was—

MYRTLE: Before you say anything, I should tell you that the pastor doesn't usually preach that long. That was a . . . that was a fluke, that's what that was.

LORI: I see.

MYRTLE: And the choir . . . well, the music minister has been sick the last couple of weeks, so they were . . . *(a "so-so" gesture.)*

LORI: Oh, I thought they were—

MYRTLE: But the special duet at the offering! Now, wasn't that wonderful!

LORI: Yes, that was just—

MYRTLE: Dorothy and Norma. Two of the sweetest gals you ever did see. And what voices! Just giving that talent up to the Lord. Do you sing?

LORI: Huh?

MYRTLE: Do you sing, Linda?

LORI *(letting it pass):* Ah . . . yes. I mean, a little. Back in high school I was in the—

MYRTLE: Oh, you've had training! We can always use people with training, you know. *(Leaning in.)* Honestly, most of the choir have so-so voices, but a lot of commitment! And that's what it's all about, isn't it? Oh, they could use someone like you up there. Alto? Soprano?

LORI: Uh, soprano. I think.

MYRTLE: You know, I should tell the music minister, Vernon Kitsch, about you! Do you mind, dear? They could really use the folks, what with the Christmas cantata coming up and all.

LORI: Well, I'm really not sure I'm good enough to—

MYRTLE *(clapping her hands):* Oh, they're going to love you, Lisa!

LORI *(wanly):* Well . . .

MYRTLE: And what about Sunday School, dear?

LORI *(backing away):* Oh, no . . . I really don't think I'm qualified to teach Sunday—

MYRTLE: Oh, no, dear! *(Laughs and takes LORI's hand.)* You are a caution! No, I mean, did you go to Sunday School? You know, this morning.

LORI *(laughing nervously):* Oh. Ah, no, I didn't. You see, I was so late I just decided to go to—

MYRTLE: Well, we just have the most wonderful Sunday School classes designed for just about anybody! *(Leans closer.)* Real up-to-date stuff, you know. You're married, aren't you.

LORI: What . . . ? Oh, yes. Yes, I—

MYRTLE *(writes in her Day Runner):* Well, "Young Marrieds," that's the class for you. Now, I'm going to tell the teacher, Mr. Heckle, that you'll be in his class next . . . oh . . . *(sighs, uncomfortably)* . . . wait a minute here. Hold everything a moment. Do you have kids?

LORI *(brightening):* I sure do. I have a baby daughter named—

MYRTLE: Uh-huh. Well. That does change everything, you know. You see, that puts you in the "Little Miracles New Parents Class" and that meets in the . . . *(clears her throat, nervously)* . . . Oh . . . I . . . well, I noticed your husband isn't here with you this morning.

LORI *(embarrassed):* Well, no . . . you see, he's really not interested in—

MYRTLE *(patting LORI's hand, gravely):* Oh, I understand completely, dear. Our men can be so . . . stiff-necked sometimes, can't they. But that would put you in the "Young Mothers with Unsaved Husbands" class.

LORI: I see.

MYRTLE *(writing in her Day Runner):* Now that's Fanny Vandersma's class. I'll let her know to look for you next week, LuLu.

LORI: Ah, my name's—

MYRTLE *(snapping the book shut):* What's that?

LORI: Never mind.

MYRTLE: Now, if you have a minute, dear, I'd like to fill you in on what our church has to offer by way of programs. *(Hands LORI a pamphlet that unfolds to the floor.)* Oh, I think you'll really love what we have going on here—oh, that reminds me, dear, do give me your address before you go. I'd like to put you on the Women's Church Mice Fellowship Newsletter mailing list. That way you'll know about everything we busy bees are planning, hmmm?

LORI: Ah . . . thank you, but I'm really just interested in—

MYRTLE *(referring to her Day Runner):* Now, let me see. Tonight, of course, is the Sunday evening service. Afterward the Church Mice all go out to Muriel Colander's restaurant for pie. We always do that. Any chance we can get, anyway. Now, Monday night is our Church Mice Boutique and Quilting Party. You'll love that. The fellowship! Remember to bring your remnants, dear. On Tuesday nights it's the women's Bible Study. I'll get you the book we're using: *Submission: Just Do It.* Wednesday nights, of course, we have our all-church programs. Bring your son to that, dear. That's the night we have our BWANA Club. That's "Boys With A New Attitude." And Thursday nights we have our choir practice, you remember. Now, let me see . . . have I told you about—oh, yes! On every second Saturday morning we cook, serve, and clean up for the Men's Fellowship Breakfast. And on the third and fourth Saturday evenings we host the all-church potluck where we Church Mice cook, serve, and clean up again. Do you cook, dear? Never you mind. You can carry a plate and wash a pot, can't you! *(Writes in her notebook.)* I'll let Grace know about that. Now, on the fourth and seventh Saturday mornings, we ladies get together for the study: "Your Marriage: More Quality Time at Home." I'll make sure you get the workbook for that one, Lena!

LORI: LORI!

MYRTLE *(confused):* Oh, no, dear . . . *(shakes LORI's hand)* . . . it's Myrtle. Myrtle Fetschwanger.

LORI: No! My name is Lori!

MYRTLE *(lost):* I'm sorry . . . I thought I already asked you what your—

LORI: You did!

MYRTLE: Well, I thought so! Anyway, I'm just so excited you're going to be attending here! Please make sure to write your name and address in the guest book for our newsletter! Oh, I just know you're going to love it here. So much to do! So many programs! You'll have no trouble serving the Lord here, dear. *(Putting away her Day Runner.)* And I do look forward to meeting that husband and son of yours. Let's see if we can't just get them here next Sunday, hmmm? Well, I'm off. I've just got an afternoon full of meetings! Make sure you meet Pastor Dorcus on your way out. *(Waving as she goes out.)* God bless, Lorna!

LORI: IT'S LORI!!

(PASTOR DORCUS *comes in.*)

PASTOR: Well, hello there, Lori!

(LORI *wheels around.*)

LORI *(barking):* WHAT?!

PASTOR *(startled):* I . . . ah . . . just said, "Hello, Lori." Didn't I hear you say . . . ? *(Holds out his hand.)* Pastor Dorcus here.

LORI *(backing away):* Yeah, whaddayou want?

PASTOR *(confused):* Oh . . . ah, well . . . say, you're new here, aren't you?

LORI: What about it!

PASTOR: Well, I . . . ah, welcome! You know, if you have just a moment, I'd love to tell you about some of our programs—

(LORI *screams and throws her bulletin in the air. She dashes off.* PASTOR DORCUS *watches the bulletin inserts flutter to the floor. A beat.*)

PASTOR: The sermon. I knew it! I knew it was too long.

(*Blackout.*)

And with Pew Commentary by Bob and Edith

A Sketch on Church Discontentment

Cast

EDITH: a woman in her 30s to 50s
BOB: her husband, a man in his 30s to 50s

Scene

A church sanctuary

Costume

Modern. Sunday best.

Props

Pew
Bible
2 hymnals

Running Time

6 minutes

Production Notes

Bob can't find it in his heart to cut slack to anyone. He remembers every wrong ever done to him, and he's awfully quick to judge, grumble, and criticize.

But he sure can find Bible verses fast.

Bob and Edith are two outrageous characters who just can't seem to find a church that lives up to their standards. As soon as the Body of Christ reveals the flesh and blood it's made up of, they are off to find greener pastures. Or is that *pastors*.

"And with Pew Commentary by Bob and Edith" is another static sketch with regards to the physical movement. The dialogue is very short and snappy, so don't lag on picking up cues. Much of the humor is in the rhythms.

Play the sketch as forward as possible. They can steal glances now and again to make the connections. The hymn music can be either taped or live.

(An organ plays a hymn in the darkness for a few moments. Perhaps "It Is Well with My Soul" or "Wonderful Peace." Lights. A church sanctuary. BOB and EDITH, dressed in their Sunday best, are standing in front of their pew finishing the hymn. They are obviously not happy. BOB flashes someone an acid look.)

BOB *(whispered)*: Would you pick it up, Anderson! *(To EDITH.)* The old bird's always five words behind on every hymn! Drives me crazy. Somebody ought to—

(The organ stops. Sudden silence.)

—take away his hymnal!

(BOB smiles sheepishly and they both sit.)

BOB/EDITH *(all smiles)*: Good morning, Pastor!

(BOB and EDITH look ahead as they speak, with quick glances to one another now and again.)

BOB *(groaning)*: Do you hear that, Edith? I knew it! Pastor's going to tell another one'a his "funny" stories. You know what? I'll bet he's only trying to fill time. I'll bet he never even started writing this sermon until he was on his way over here for services this morning. You know what I mean? Isn't that just like him?

EDITH: You know, I think that man has put on some weight again. What do you think? Somebody ought to tell that man he's a bad witness.

BOB: C'mon, Pastor! Time to change the oil! For the love'a Mike! The man's had the same hairstyle since 1963.

(BOB and EDITH laugh. BOB slaps his knee.)

BOB: Why are we laughing at that? It's not even that funny. Just another one of his cornpone stories.

EDITH: That story was better than last week's. I think.

BOB (*looking around*): Look at these people, Edith! Just smiling away. They don't know what their shepherd is *really* like.

EDITH: Oh, quick, Bob! Pastor just gave the Scripture reading! Ephesians 4:25-32! Look it up!

(BOB *whips open his Bible and shuffles through the pages. He looks up, smiling.*)

EDITH: You are so fast, Bob. You're the first one there. You're always the first one there.

BOB (*looking around*): Yeah. Look at Charlie Schnooker over there. His Bible's all rigged up with those tabs and all. He couldn't find Ephesians with two hands and a map! (*Pause.*) Why are we still going here, Edith? We don't belong in this church.

EDITH: Why'd we leave the last church and come here, that's what I'd like to know? We really liked the other church.

BOB: That other pastor. I'm tellin' you, he was a spiritual man.

EDITH: A real man of God.

BOB: Now, he cared about people.

EDITH: If you missed a service, that man would be right on the phone asking if you were all right.

BOB: Now this guy here, he'd wait till you missed a month, then he'd make a note to call you and he'd *lose* it.

EDITH: You know, Bob. I'll bet he never gives us a thought all week.

BOB: He's *never* given us a thought, Edith. Do you remember when we invited him over for dinner? He was an hour late. An *hour* late!

EDITH: He told us he was trying to talk some girl out of committing suicide!

BOB: Ha! I never believed that one.

EDITH: I mean, even if he was, he could have said to her, "Can you hold on just a minute?" and given us a call.

BOB: An hour late. An hour late!

EDITH: My kidney pie was like rubber.

BOB: But we showed him, didn't we? I haven't shook his hand ever since.

EDITH: We've been civil.

BOB: We've been fair.

EDITH: We've kept up our attendance.

BOB: We've kept up our tithe.

EDITH: We've even kept up our smile.

BOB: But we will *never* shake his hand!

(They nod. Small pause.)

EDITH: The fellowship was better over at the other church too.

BOB: So were the coffee hours.

EDITH: I liked their choir much better.

BOB *(squirming):* The pews were more comfortable.

EDITH: You know . . . they just *did* more.

BOB: They had more . . . programs.

EDITH: More potlucks.

BOB: More cantatas.

EDITH: More fund-raisers.

BOB: They knew how to do things right over there!

(Beat.)

EDITH: Then why are we still here?

BOB: I wish we could go back there, Edith.

EDITH: But why can't we?

BOB: Because we told that other pastor off, remember?

EDITH: That's right! In front of the all-church meeting.

BOB: I'd be too embarrassed to go back now, Edith.

EDITH: Oh, I'm sure he's forgiven you by now. That's the kind of man he is. *(Beat.)* What'd he do, anyways?

BOB: Well, he only forgot to come to your second cousin's birthday, that's all.

EDITH: That's right. And after I invited him special.

BOB: He let us down. He eroded our trust.

EDITH: And after he said he'd try to come after the four weddings, two funerals, a prayer breakfast, and a missions conference he had that same weekend.

BOB: Then he turned down one of my suggestions. Remember that? He turned it down flat. He asked my opinion and I told him straight out, "I think the church should be painted brown and fuchsia, not brown and gold."

EDITH: He didn't even consider it, did he? I'll bet he wasn't even listening.

BOB: So I showed him. I sat in the front row every Sunday, and I made sure I never looked at him. Through the whole sermon. Ewww, everybody knew I was boiling!

EDITH: You told him he wasn't fit to serve.

BOB: He wasn't a man of God!

EDITH: He made too many mistakes.

BOB: Had too many shortcomings.

EDITH: He lost our respect.

BOB: I can't believe the man's still a pastor! *(A beat.)* You know what, Edith? I'll bet these two guys went to the same seminary, what d'you think?

EDITH: I'll bet they're good friends too.

BOB: I'll bet this pastor told that other pastor all the things we told this pastor about the other pastor.

EDITH: This pastor would do that!

BOB: And I'll bet that other pastor told this pastor that we we're comin' here and to watch out for the troublemakers. They're together in this. I know it!

EDITH: Why can't they act like the men of God they went to seminary to be!

BOB: I just don't think I can stand it here any longer, Edith!

EDITH: Not under these ungodly conditions.

BOB: You're so right! *(He stands.)* We're going to find ourselves . . . A BETTER CHURCH!

EDITH *(aghast):* Right in the middle of the sermon, Bob?

BOB: That's right, Edith! I want *everybody* to see us go! *(A beat. He looks around, sheepishly. He sits.)* Ah . . . maybe we're being a tad too quick to judge.

EDITH: You may be right, Bob.

BOB: Maybe we should give this a little more thought. *(A beat.)* Okay, I've thought about it. I'm going to give this pastor just one more chance. One more. If he doesn't straighten up and fly right, well—

EDITH: We'll pray about it.

BOB: A'course we'll pray about it! But then we're outta here!

EDITH *(patting):* I think that's the godly thing to do, dear.

BOB: You bet.

(*They nod. A beat.* BOB *sinks down in the pew and fold his arms, sulking.*)

BOB: Still not gonna shake his hand.

(*Blackout.*)

Opening Night at the Baptistry

A Sketch on Baptism

Cast

PHIL: a man in his 20s to 30s
JOHN: a man in his 20s to 40s

Scene

A robe room off a baptismal tank

Props

Freestanding rack of baptismal robes
Mirror (optional)
Metal folding chairs

Costumes

Baptismal robes

Running Time

7-8 minutes

Production Notes

"Opening Night at the Baptistry" is not meant to make fun of the sacrament of baptism. The intention is to find humor and education from two very different views of the event. John has trouble seeing baptism as a significant step in a Christian's life. Phil thinks it's too significant—for others, that is. Baptism, for him, is an act that convinces others of your spirituality, not a personal, sure-footed step toward God.

The hymn at the beginning of the sketch can either be taped or played live. If your church sprinkles instead of immerses, you might have to do some re-writing.

(In the darkness, an organ is playing the hymn "Peace, Perfect Peace" for a few moments. Lights. A small room off a baptistry. A rack of robes, a mirror, metal folding chairs, and stairs leading up to the baptismal tank, left. PHIL and JOHN are waiting to be baptized. Both wear white robes. PHIL is pacing, terrified, and looking up at the stairs. JOHN watches him, leaning back in his chair. The hymn fades out.)

JOHN *(after a few moments)*: Would you siddown!

(PHIL immediately drops into a seat next to JOHN. A beat. PHIL begins drumming on his knee. Then bounces his leg. JOHN watches him with increased irritation. Soon PHIL has become a mess of bopping and tapping.)

JOHN: Would you pace!

(PHIL shoots to his feet and paces.)

JOHN: Phil, you're not nervous or anything, are you?

PHIL *(too fast)*: No!

JOHN: Well, that's a relief. I was afraid you might have an anxiety attack out there or something and drown.

PHIL: Well, that calmed me down.

JOHN: It was only a joke.

PHIL: A joke? John, I really want this thing to go smooth, you know? I want to make sure it's perfect. I don't want any . . . complications.

JOHN: Phil. Your wife's not having a baby in the next room, for cryin' out loud. It's just a baptism!

PHIL: *Just* a baptism? *Just* a baptism?! Listen to him. Did Jesus say, "Oh, go ahead, John, it's *just* a baptism"? Did the Ethiopian eunuch say, "That little pond? Ah, no big deal. It's *only* a baptism"?

JOHN: Okay. I'm sorry. *(He goes and looks up the stairs toward the baptismal tank.)*

PHIL: I've been waiting a long time for this. My whole family's out there. Heathen and all. Aunt Bumiller's out there. Aunt Bumiller who always handed out tracts on Halloween instead of candy is sitting out there in the front row. John, she's been praying for this for 10 years.

JOHN: Well, she better keep praying.

PHIL: What's wrong?

JOHN: They're dunkin' the fat lady.

PHIL (coming to the stairs): You mean Mrs. Vanderlipps.

(They watch for a moment.)

JOHN: Hoo, boy.

PHIL: Was she supposed to splash like that?

JOHN: She took out half the choir.

(A beat.)

PHIL: How long is she gonna stay under?

JOHN: You know what they say. It's not over till the fat lady drowns.

PHIL: What?!

JOHN (grabs PHIL's arm and pulls him away): Look, I don't think you should be watching the other people.

PHIL (wringing his hands): Wow. Maybe I'm not ready for this, huh? Maybe I'm not spiritually prepared. Maybe I should lose a little weight.

JOHN: Knock it off. You'll do fine.

(PHIL starts reading the palm of his hand, mumbling quietly to himself.)

PHIL: I haven't been this nervous since the time I played dental floss in third grade. I've been rehearsing my testimony all week. I want to make sure I don't leave anything out—

JOHN: What's on your hand?

PHIL (innocently): Uh, my hand?

JOHN: C'mon, Phil. Lemme see the hand.

(PHIL opens his hand, sheepishly.)

JOHN: Notes! The man has his entire life written on the palm of his hands.

PHIL: Well, I didn't want to forget!

JOHN: What? Your lines?

PHIL: No. My faith journey. I didn't want to leave anything—

JOHN: Phil, this is a baptism. What happens in a baptism?

PHIL: What do you mean? You get baptized—no! You get wet!

JOHN: Most people do.

PHIL: Water . . . wet! The ink'll wash off!

JOHN: Mind like a steel trap.

PHIL: Swirls of ink floating off my body, turning the baptismal waters black. Ohhh, that won't look good. I can see it now. The pastor'll think it's a sign from God.

(PHIL *starts wiping his hand on his robe. It leaves smudges.*)

JOHN: Phil. The robe.

PHIL *(looking down):* Oh, no. Oh, no! I ruined a baptismal robe. "Man Vandalizes Own Baptismal Robe," "Demon Possession Suspected." I can see where this evening's headed.

JOHN: Would you just relax! Everything'll go fine, okay? Just peachy. Trust me. There's nothing to it.

PHIL: And how d'you know that? You're in here with me! You have no idea!

JOHN *(vaguely):* I just . . . know, okay?

PHIL: What do you mean? Wait a minute, is God revealing something to you I should know? Tell me!

JOHN: Phil, I just know about these things, okay! Look, forget I even—

PHIL: Hold on. Time out. You've done this before, haven't you? You've been dunked before, and you're holding out on me!

JOHN: Where'd you get that idea . . . I . . . *(sighs)* . . . okay, okay. I've done this before. Maybe once.

PHIL: Once?

JOHN: Or twice.

PHIL: TWICE!

JOHN: Okay! Twice!

PHIL: You're telling me this is your *third* dive? What happened? You backslid *that* bad? Twice?

JOHN: No, I . . . well, the first time was when I was a baby.

PHIL: Yeah?

JOHN: So I don't even remember it!

PHIL: So what happened the second time? Amnesia again?

JOHN: No. I did it to impress my girlfriend.

PHIL: You couldn't have just taken her out to a nice restaurant?

JOHN: She was the pastor's daughter. It was the most impressive thing I could think of.

PHIL: Did it work?

JOHN: The impression or the baptism?

PHIL: Oh. She dumped you.

JOHN: Yeah! She dumped me, okay! So now, tonight, this one's for me. All me.

PHIL: And God.

JOHN: And God, yeah! Of course "and God." What do you think I am, some kind'a heathen?

PHIL: I don't know. I'm not the one who's needed three baptisms.

JOHN: Yeah? And who's pacing the floor terrified about forgetting his lines for the big opening!

PHIL: This is different. I want to—

JOHN: Make a good impression. I know.

(A beat. PHIL *paces.)*

PHIL: Does the water go up your nose?

JOHN: What?

PHIL: You've done this before. Does the water go up your nose?

JOHN: No, Phil. The pastor holds your nose.

PHIL: He holds you by the nose!

JOHN: Weren't you listening in baptism class?

PHIL: The water's not going to be freezing, is it?

JOHN: The pastor told you it would be heated.

PHIL: That's what he *tells* you. But maybe they really keep it ice cold. You know, to test your faith or something. The final big faith test. Maybe I'll wade out there and say something stupid like—AGGGGHHHHHH!

JOHN *(looking up the stairs):* Me? *(Nods.)* Okay. *(To* PHIL.*)* Look, I'm on—I mean, they're ready for me. Relax. Please. You're going to be fine. You know, you're taking this thing way too seriously. *(He goes out.)*

PHIL: Too seriously? It's a baptism! How am I supposed to take it? It's a one-shot deal. I don't want to blow it out there. I want to be a good witness. Besides, if I mess up, Aunt Bumiller's going to make me read the collected works of Oswald Chambers. Again. *(Takes a deep breath.)* Okay, calm down.

Just calm yourself down. *(Another deep breath.)* John's right. It'll all turn out just fine. I wonder if my testimony's too long? It might look like spiritual pride. Maybe I should leave out the part about the theological significance of the crafts I made at Happydale Christian Camp. *(Looks up the stairs.)* Oh, brother. I'm a wreck. An absolute wreck. *(Looks around. Panics.)* Where's my clothes?! Where's my—?! Oh, no! *(Clutches his robe.)* I'll have to drive home in this. "Man Steals Wet Baptismal Robe," "Backsliding Suspected." *(He finds a stack of clothes on a chair.)* That's right. I put 'em there. *(Goes to the stairs.)* God, help me not to blow it out there. Help me to . . . *(He goes wide-eyed.)* What's he looking at? *(Points to himself.)* Me? A-All right. *(Deep breath.)* Okay, okay. Here goes. *(Starts up the stairs.)* God, help me . . . God, help me to remember . . . God, help me to remember . . . *(Stops.)* Help me to remember You.

(He goes off as the lights fade to:

(Blackout.)

A Peace of Christ

A Sketch on Reconciliation for Communion

Cast

FRANK: a man in his 30s to 60s
GEORGE: a man in his 30s to 60s

Scene

A church sanctuary

Props

Chairs or pews
4 Communion trays (optional)

Costumes

Sunday suits

Running Time

5 minutes

Production Notes

This sketch is based on Matthew 5:23-24 and 1 Corinthians 11:23-30, verses about the importance of self-examination and reconciliation when coming to the table of the Lord. Scripture makes it clear that if we come to Communion quarreling and judging others, we will bring judgment down on ourselves.

George and Frank are both nursing a long-forgotten grudge. As they serve Communion, they each move from bitterness to accusation, then from remorse to grace and on to personal responsibility and reconciliation.

This sketch can either be performed on a playing area or in the actual aisles of the sanctuary, passing real Communion trays through the audience. If you choose the latter option, you will probably need to use radio mikes. Make sure to set up the fact that George and Frank are speaking their thoughts and not talking to each other.

The hymn music can either be live or taped. Tape will probably give you more flexibility with the sound.

(The hymn "Jesus Paid It All" is heard in the darkness for a few moments. Lights. A church sanctuary. Chairs face downstage toward the pulpit. FRANK and GEORGE, two ushers, mime passing a Communion tray down the rows. They speak their thoughts, but neither can hear.)

FRANK *(looking at GEORGE)*: What's he looking at?

GEORGE *(looking at FRANK)*: What's his problem?

FRANK: I specifically asked *not* to be put on the serving schedule with George.

GEORGE: Someone did this on purpose. I was supposed to be serving at 9:30.

(They catch each other's eyes and smile.)

FRANK: There he goes with that Broadway smile. Good Ol' George. Always here for Communion Sunday. Always here for potlucks. But let there be a workday? "Where's George?"

GEORGE: Oh, boy. Frank's got his "holy face" on. Holier than thous, more like it. What's it been now, Frank? Two, three Sundays you missed. But always here on Communion night. Can't backslide completely, now can we?

FRANK: Know what irritates me about George? Always complaining at church meetings. Sits there and shoots down everybody's ideas like clay pigeons.

GEORGE: Know what really gets my goat? Frank's negative attitude. Forever griping about what needs to get done, then sitting on his duff.

FRANK: You know, it's people like George that make me dread coming to worship.

GEORGE: You know, it's people like Frank that keep folks away from churches.

(They have finished passing out the Communion bread. They take the trays to the pulpit and hand them to the "minister." The organ stops playing. FRANK and GEORGE take a Communion bread.)

FRANK/GEORGE: Sure glad I'm not a hypocrite. Like him.

   (They look at each other.)

   "Do this in remembrance of me."

(They put the bread in their mouths. The organ starts playing "Nothing but the Blood." FRANK and GEORGE take the "trays" of cups.)

FRANK: What happened to you, George?

GEORGE *(same time):* What happened to you, Frank?

(They start passing the "trays" down the rows.)

GEORGE: I remember when I used to look up to you. You seemed like you had it all together. Now my stomach twists into a knot every time I see you.

FRANK: One of the reasons Ellie and me stayed here so long was because of you and Elaine. You were so friendly. Cared about us from the beginning. Now I can get irritated just looking at you.

FRANK/GEORGE: When did that start happening?

(They catch each other's eyes. Sad smiles.)

GEORGE: Boy, did I just have a memory. Remember when we planned that "Italian Night" fund-raiser? Nobody came, and we all ate spaghetti for lunch for about six months!

FRANK: You know, I can still remember fishing over July Fourth weekend. Waking up and doing devotions at sunrise. Eating tuna sandwiches because we didn't catch anything but ticks.

GEORGE: You came over and checked on me every day for two weeks while I was in the worst of my pneumonia.

FRANK: All those "anonymous" checks in my mailbox when I was out of work.

GEORGE: Now we only see each other at church events. Even then we avoid each other.

FRANK: Make sure we're not in the same discussion groups.

FRANK/GEORGE: What did you do to hurt me?

FRANK: I really don't remember exactly what it was. Maybe it was a lot of things put together.

GEORGE: Maybe it was nothing.

(They glance at each other.)

FRANK: Was it my fault? Did I expect too much out of you?

GEORGE: Was it me? Did I put you up on a pedestal?

(They walk up the aisle toward the "minister.")

FRANK: I wonder if he remembers what we're really fighting about?

GEORGE: I wonder if he knows why we're so mad at each other?

(*They hand up the "trays" and take a cup for themselves.*)

FRANK/GEORGE: Maybe I should ask him.

    (*They face each other with the cups.*)

    The peace of Christ.

(*They freeze with hands up, holding the cups. The lights fade to:*)

(*Blackout.*)

PART TWO:

DRAMATIC RESOURCES FOR SPECIAL DAYS IN THE CHURCH

Attempted to Deliver

A Monologue for Christmas

Cast

UPS WORKER: a woman or man of any age

Scene

UPS warehouse

Props

Packages of all shapes, sizes

Costume

UPS uniform

Running Time

5 minutes

Production Notes

"I hope you're beginning to catch some of the spiritual shadings of some of the stuff I'm talking about here."

These are the words of the UPS Worker in the Christmas monologue "Attempted to Deliver," where we are taken through a tour of the Dead-end Room

73

of gifts that, for one reason or another, were not able to get through to the recipient.

Some moved and left no forwarding address, some received notices and promised to pick up their packages, but never did. And some were never interested in getting their gift in the first place.

"Attempted to Deliver" is a fourth-wall-breaker of a monologue where the actor is talking directly to the audience, even bringing them into the scene. It needs to feel very natural and folksy.

Take your time. And feel free to work out more bits with the packages stacked all around.

(Lights. The Dead-end Room of a UPS office, where misaddressed or unclaimed Christmas packages go to wait. Stacks of brown-wrapped packages in heaps and piles around the playing area. We can hear distant Christmas Muzak, coming from a radio or something. UPS WORKER comes in, carrying a huge stack of packages. He's trying to be careful but steps on a stray package and slips. The boxes he's carrying crash to the floor. UPS WORKER just stands there, staring at piles of packages.)

UPS WORKER: We try to be as careful as we can. Seriously. *(Picks up the packages and puts them on stacks.)* But mail is up 50 percent at Christmas. 50 percent! That's like . . . well, if you typed 20 letters a day, now you're typing 40. Or, if you had 9 tables in your section and now you've got 18! And every single person at every single table wants a separate check. You can get a little bushed by the end of the day, as you can probably imagine.

(He's come to the last package. He hears something. He shakes the box. Whatever was inside was made of glass—and it isn't in one piece anymore.)

Uh-oh. This happens once in a while. Seriously. Usually when you hear something like this . . . *(shakes the box of broken glass)* . . . it just means the contents were packed wrong. People don't pack things as well as they could.

(He tosses the box across the room onto a pile. It makes a horrible crash.)

Well, Merry Christmas! *(Comes down into the audience.)* What are all of you doing here anyway? You should be standing in line at the post office! No, no, just kidding. I know you've all been smart and mailed your gifts out weeks ago. *(He looks at an audience member.)* Maybe you're not as smart as you look. *(Takes in a deep breath.)* Well, you know, some people believe that you can give gifts up to 12 days *after* Christmas. I'm sure if you mailed it now we could get it there sometime in January. Seriously.

(Goes back up into the playing area.)

Look around you. This here is something you don't get to see very often. This room is what you might call the "underbelly" of the postal business. This . . . is the Dead-end Room. Sounds like a Stephen King novel, doesn't it?

(He moves around the room picking up packages.)

This is a sad place. All these packages here? All these Christmas gifts? These are the dead-end packages. For some reason or another, every package you see here is undeliverable. Tripped up in transit. Marooned in motion. You might say—all addressed up and no place to go. *(Laughs.)* See, if you look closely, the story of what Christmas is really all about can be found in this room. I'll show you.

(Picks up a package.)

Look at this one here. Here's a package that won't be here long. The person sending this Christmas gift had the wrong address. Pure and simple. No such person at that address, so we just send it back to the sender and they can figure out what went wrong and all. Check their records or call the person and get the right address. Happy ending and Merry Christmas. Okay.

(Picks up another one.)

Okay, this gift *tried* to get through. It really did. Right address, right name, right zip. The whole works. What do you think went wrong? No one by that name lives there anymore. That's right. They're gone. And there's no forwarding address. They didn't bother to tell anyone where they were going, and so they lost out on . . . *(shakes the package)* . . . you wanna take a guess?

(He hands the package to an audience member.)

You know what that is? No? It's a fruit cake. Seriously. Well, it's either fruit cake or fine bone china. It's one of the two. You get to know these things.

(Takes the package back.)

The thing is, we can't keep track of everybody who moves. There's only one person that can do that. And don't say the IRS. See, the bottom line is, you've got to want to be found. You've got to want contact. If the gift goes out, and you're in hiding, it's going to have to go back to the sender. *(A beat.)* I hope you're beginning to catch the spiritual shadings of what I'm talking about here. If not, now's the time to start.

(He drops the package on a pile. It hits with a heavy thud. He smiles.)

Definitely fruit cake. Seriously.

(Picks up another package.)

You ever come home and see one of those yellow tags on your door. "We'll try again" postcards. You know, the ones where you go out for two minutes and come back and there it is. "Hey, I just went to take the garbage out!" Anyway, that's what happened to this gift. We make a couple of trips out, the person's never there, but they call and say, "Hold it for me." And we do. We hold it. But they forget about it, they get sidetracked with all the other stuff at Christmas, and they never get down to the office to get it. So, it goes back to the sender. That person never even knows what he could have had, you know. What if this was the gift to end all Christmas gifts, huh? How will they ever know? I suppose they could call the sender and ask them to send it back, right? It's never too late for that. *(Smiles.)* Keep up with me, now. Spiritually speaking.

(Picks up another package.)

Now, this makes me the most sad of all. I look at these packages come through, and I get very, very sad. Especially at Christmastime. See this? The sender took time on this gift, sent it out knowing what it would mean to the receiver—and they never picked it up. Never called to say, "Hold it for me." Never took the time. Didn't care. Didn't want it. Maybe didn't think it was anything special. Made their mind up already that it wasn't important. They saw the notices, maybe all streaked with rain or flapping in the cold wind, and they tore them up. Crunched them up and threw them in the trash can. So, what do you think about that? I see it all the time here. It makes me so sad.

(Sets the package down, gently.)

I mean, who did all the work to send it, huh? All they had to do was reach out and take it. That's all. Reach out, grab hold, open it up. Now, it has to go back. Unopened. Tell me, if you sent someone a gift like this, and it came back untouched, how would you feel? I can tell you, it would kill me. *(A beat.)* Seriously.

(Blackout.)

Shopper's Suite

A Sketch with Carols for Christmas

Cast

The cast for "Shopper's Suite" is made up of adult and children's choirs who play all the acting parts.

LONE SHOPPER

MOTHER

MOTHER TWO

FATHER

CLERK

UPSET SHOPPER

SHOPPER ONE

SHOPPER TWO

SHOPPER THREE

CHILD WITH A BALLOON

CHILD TWO

BOY ONE

GIRL TWO

PIANIST

Scene

A mall

Props

Balloon
Shopping bags
Shopping lists

Costumes

Modern

Running Time

12-15 minutes

Production Notes

"Shopper's Suite" is designed as a carol/drama mix for either a church or neutral setting—a banquet, a concert, or a mall (in this case you'll have to use an electric piano or synthesizer). The play was created with the idea of having a church choir either perform the acting themselves or bring in actors from the church to fill in their ranks.

Carols found in any hymnal were chosen for the sketch, mainly because they're in public domain. If you prefer to use other Christmas songs or original music, please feel free to substitute them. These might actually be closer to the spirit of the sketches and monologues.

(A mall. Christmas Muzak. The sound of shoppers, registers, phones. A single weary LONE SHOPPER *comes in, loaded with bags. With a heavy sigh,* LONE SHOPPER *sets down her stuff. Pulls a list out of her pocket and checks it over. Sighs, shakes her head.* LONE SHOPPER *sings, a cappella, the first verse of:)*

>"O Come, All Ye Faithful"

(As LONE SHOPPER *begins the chorus, a few voices begin to join her. Then more. Finally, up the aisles, come a host of* SHOPPERS, *all singing the chorus. Several of them have children in tow. They join* LONE SHOPPER *at the playing area and finish the carol.*

(At the close, the SHOPPERS *immediately break into a fury of buying vignettes. Loud, furious, and anxious. Some haggle over the same item. Some argue with clerks and cashiers. Others shout at their children or spouses. The* PIANIST *begins playing Tchaikovsky's "Dance of the Sugar Plum Fairies," very softly.*

(A MOTHER *dragging* CHILD WITH A BALLOON *walks past. The* MOTHER *is furious, the child looks completely demoralized.)*

MOTHER: I told you I don't have time to mess with you tonight! I don't want to hear another word out of you! Straighten up! I should have left you in the car!

(As they cross the playing area, the CHILD WITH A BALLOON *stops. The* MOTHER *continues on, hand outstretched behind her, as if her child were still with her. She rants until she is off.* CHILD WITH A BALLOON *stands there, looking down at the ground, sadly. Immediately,* MOTHER TWO *walks past with* CHILD TWO. *She walks a few feet ahead, stern and focused.* CHILD TWO *has her hands out, pretending to touch all the merchandise.)*

CHILD TWO *(chanting):* Don't toouuch anything! Don't toouuch anything! Don't toouuch anything! Don't toouuch anything!

*(*CHILD TWO *stops at the* CHILD WITH A BALLOON. MOTHER TWO *continues off-stage, oblivious.* CHILD TWO *and* CHILD WITH A BALLOON *look at each other. They*

both look up at the balloon. Immediately, an impatient FATHER *barrels past with two children,* BOY ONE *yanking on* GIRL TWO's *arm.*)

BOY ONE: You wanna spanking?!

GIRL TWO: No!

BOY ONE: You wanna spanking?!

GIRL TWO: No!

BOY ONE: You wanna spanking?!

GIRL TWO: No!

(These two also stop at center with the other children, looking at the balloon. The harried FATHER *walks on. Everyone freezes, except the children.)*

CHILD WITH A BALLOON: What did they say to you?

CHILD TWO: She said if I touched anything, oooone thing! There'd be nuthin' for me under the Christmas tree. Not oooone thing!

BOY ONE: He said he was sorry he brought us along. We were both in his way. He should'a left us at Gramma's. You wanna spanking?!

GIRL TWO: NO!

CHILD WITH A BALLOON: My mom told me if I wanted to live to see Christmas, I better not make a peep.

GIRL TWO: Did you?

CHILD WITH A BALLOON: No way! And I had to peep all night!

CHILD TWO: Where'd you get that balloon?

CHILD WITH A BALLOON: This man was handin' 'em out. I really wanted it. My mom said I could have it if I SHUT up, didn't BUG her, and didn't say ANOTHER WORD to her for the REST OF THE NIGHT.
(A beat.)
I don't like Christmas anymore.

*(*CHILD WITH A BALLOON *holds up the balloon and lets it go. They all watch it float to the ceiling.* CHILD WITH A BALLOON, CHILD TWO, BOY ONE, *and* GIRL TWO *sing the first verse of:)*

"Away in a Manger"

(At the beginning of the second verse, CHILDREN *come up the aisles and join them in the front to sing the rest of the carol. At the close, the whole scene unfreezes.* SHOPPERS *and* CHILDREN *sing:)*

"Angels We Have Heard on High"

(At the close of the carol, the SHOPPERS *break into the buying melee again, as before. Noisy and furious. A* CLERK *suddenly steps away from an* UPSET SHOPPER *and walks toward the audience. She looks almost as if she's in a dream.)*

CLERK: Stop, please!

(The SHOPPERS *continue their frenzy, only in mime.* CLERK *looks around. The* PIANIST *begins to play carols, softly in the background.)*

That's what I want to say sometimes. Just stop. Everyone go home. Watch the "Grinch," sing "Wahoo, Doray." Make brownies. Sing carols. Make each other gifts out of yarn and paper and . . . glue and . . . Popsicle sticks!

(A deep breath. She calms down.)

It's ridiculous to wish that. I know it. Shopping . . . That's all part of it, isn't it? I mean, I like seeing my family ooo and ahh over the gifts I bought them. Who wouldn't? It's as much a part of the season as "Silent Night." Well, isn't it? You know, I took this sales job three years ago. Every Christmas for three years I get this extra job just to pay for Christmas. Spending cash. That's the gift I give myself now.

(Pause.)

I'm going to be real honest. This mall has ruined Christmas for me. Well, maybe not completely. But I sure don't wake up on Christmas morning with the same feeling. Even the carols aren't the same. I hear "Joy to the World," and I remember that's the time this yuppie couple screamed in my face because we only had the coffee grinders in black not white. They're ranting to pieces in front of me, and I'm hearing "Joy to the World" in the background. I wanted to shout at them, "Stop, please! Listen to this for a moment? Doesn't that make you glow inside?" You know, I get home near midnight and I want to count my blessings. All I can count is how many times somebody hurt my feelings that night. You get your feelings hurt a lot around here. You either get 'em hurt, or you turn into an icicle and treat every shopper like the enemy. Is getting what you want so important you have to treat me like garbage?

UPSET SHOPPER: Miss? MISS! Are you deaf? Can I get this blender in five speeds or not?!

CLERK *(to audience):* I guess it is.

(Quietly, the CLERK *sings the first verse of:)*

"Joy to the World"

(At the close of the first verse, the SHOPPERS *join in to finish the carol. This cheers* CLERK. *Then they sing:)*

"O Little Town of Bethlehem"

STORE ANNOUNCER: Good evening, shoppers. We'd like to wish you and yours a very happy holiday. Please bring your purchases to the registers. Our store is now closed.

SHOPPERS: CLOSED?!

(The PIANIST begins playing "Jingle Bells" at top speed. The SHOPPERS begin moving in an ever-quickening circle, grabbing at merchandise and throwing it in their bags. Suddenly SHOPPER ONE spins out toward the audience. SHOPPER TWO and THREE follow.)

SHOPPER ONE *(showing a list):* One more person!

SHOPPER TWO *(a list):* Eight more people!

SHOPPER THREE *(a list):* Twenty-two more people!

SHOPPERS ONE and TWO: WHAT?!

SHOPPER THREE *(sheepishly):* I just started tonight.

SHOPPER ONE: But the store's closing in five minutes.

SHOPPER TWO: And it's Christmas Eve!

SHOPPER ONE: What're you gonna do?

SHOPPER THREE: 7-11! It's open all night!

SHOPPER TWO: Can they gift-wrap a Slurpee?

SHOPPER THREE: Worth a try! Come on!

(SHOPPERS TWO and THREE turn to go. Everyone freezes. SHOPPER ONE steps toward the audience.)

SHOPPER ONE: One gift. That's all I had to find. One gift. The perfect gift. And I couldn't do it. I couldn't find it. You know what kind of gift I'm talking about, don't you? One that would . . . make a person's whole Christmas season. The whole year. Maybe something that would . . . I don't know . . . something that would really change their life. I don't know about you, but I am so sick of giving . . . ties, or CDs, or . . . what else . . . perfume. Am I the only one that feels like that? Just once, I'd like to see someone I loved get a gift that would really make a difference in their life. You know, one they'd . . . always cherish. One they could look back at and know something changed that day. A gift that, once they had it, they'd wonder how they ever lived without it. *(A tired smile.)* I'd like to get a gift like that myself.

(A beat. SHOPPER ONE heads out the aisle. Immediately, the circle of SHOPPERS begins again. Furiously grabbing at merchandise and tossing it in their bags. They begin singing:)

"We Wish You a Merry Christmas"

(The lights begin to fade as they sing, eventually taking the whole scene to:

(Blackout.)

No Room in the Ramada Inn

A Family Sketch for Christmas

Cast

RALPH: a man in his 30s or 40s
LORNA: a woman in her 30s or 40s
KYLE: a teenage boy
DANA: a teenage girl
WAITRESS: late teens, early 20s

Scene

A restaurant

Props

Table
Chairs
Dishes
Menus

Costume

Modern

Running Time

5 minutes

Production Notes

"No Room in the Ramada Inn" takes a look at what happens when one family strips away all the trimmings of Christmas and just has each other.

It's not a pleasant sight. At first, anyway.

This sketch covers a lot of emotional ground in a short space. Don't be afraid to "air it out" with pauses to make the shifts in thinking and feeling seem real.

*(In the darkness the sound of a restaurant—voices, clanking dishware, Christmas Muzak. Lights. The Lowry family—*RALPH, LORNA, DANA, *and* KYLE—*are sitting at a restaurant table that is piled high with dishes.* LORNA, DANA, *and* KYLE *are dead asleep, faces flat on the table.* RALPH *is drinking coffee.)*

RALPH: I don't know why I ever switched to decaf. This is great. I feel like a million bucks! Honey? Lorna? *(Sees she's asleep.)* Come on, honey. Sit up. Have some more coffee.

LORNA *(delirious):* No . . . no more coffee . . . please . . . don't make me do it . . . I won't be able to sleep . . . *(She falls back asleep.)*

RALPH: Kids? *(Rousing them.)* Kids, come on, huh? Don't leave dad to fly solo, huh? He needs his copilots! Come on, have some coffee. No, forget that. Coffee has too much caffeine. How about some hot chocolate! *(Signals the* WAITRESS.*)*

*(*WAITRESS *comes in, bone tired and bedraggled.)*

WAITRESS: You want a couple of pillows?

RALPH: No, just two hot chocolates.

(The WAITRESS *goes out.* RALPH *sings a carol to himself. He gets a little loud—and a little off-key. The family sits up and watches him.)*

RALPH: Yikes! Didn't know I had an audience.

LORNA: Ralph, would you quit with the Fred McMurray routine.

RALPH: Look, it's Christmas Eve, and I'm going to enjoy it. Even if we are stuck in a Dennys.

DANA: Would you get real? This is not Christmas Eve, okay? Do you see a Christmas tree? Do you see presents? Do you see your children safe in their beds with visions of sugarplums dancin' in their heads?

RALPH: There's a little Christmas tree right at the front counter over—

KYLE: Dad. Someone made it out of, like, bounced checks or something. Then they put green food dye on it.

DANA: Okay. It might be Christmas Eve for the rest of the whole entire solar system, but not for us. You do not spend Christmas Eve in a Dennys. No way. Uh-uh. I refuse to take part in the holiday.

LORNA: Come on, Dana. Your dad tried to get us a room, didn't he? Just as soon as we found out the car that only made funny noises when Mommy drove it was as dead as a doornail and couldn't get fixed until Christmas morning.

RALPH: Maybe we could all sing some carols!

(The kids groan.)

LORNA: Ralph, don't embarrass the children. It's hard on them enough as it is.

RALPH: Hard? HARD? We're sitting in this great Dennys where we can get as much wonderful food as we want. There's Christmas music playing. This is great. When I was a kid, we couldn't even afford a Christmas tree. We made one out of scraps of branches we found at the tree lot. We had to dig around in the snow.

KYLE: Snow? Dad, you grew up in San Diego.

LORNA: That was your father who dug around in the snow, Ralph.

RALPH: Oh, yeah. Well, I went without something at Christmastime. I don't remember right now what it was, but it was something.

(WAITRESS *comes in carrying the hot chocolates.)*

WAITRESS: Here's your hot chocolates. Anything else?

RALPH: A refill when you get a chance.

WAITRESS: Leaded?

LORNA: He'll have decaf, thanks.

WAITRESS: Don't want him bouncing off the Naugahyde, huh? Can I ask you a question? You all have been here since I came on shift eight hours ago. Now, I know we've got some great late-night specials, but it *is* Christmas Eve, after all.

LORNA: No room in the inn.

WAITRESS: What's that?

RALPH: Our car broke down, and we couldn't find a hotel with a room vacant.

LORNA: And the car won't be ready until noon.

KYLE: What time is it now?

WAITRESS: 5:30 A.M. *(They groan.)* I'll bring you all breakfast menus in a little while. *(She goes out.)*

DANA: Boy, this is a Christmas to remember. When I was a kid I wanted to stay up all night on Christmas. Not anymore.

LORNA: Oh, it's good practice for when you have kids.

KYLE: We didn't get to open our Christmas Eve present.

DANA: Didn't get to lie in bed and listen to you two get into a fight putting stuff together.

KYLE: And by the time we get home, I'm gonna be too tired to open my presents.

DANA: No Christmas meal. No fresh-baked cookies. No TV specials. Nothing. This is one dragoid Christmas.

KYLE: Ditto.

RALPH: Come on. We have each other, don't we? We haven't been this together on Christmas Eve since Kyle's voice changed.

KYLE: Dad!

RALPH: I don't know about you, but I'm grateful I have all of you here with me. Christmas has become kind of a dragoid for me too these last few years.

DANA: Get real.

RALPH: We do the same things, say the same things, go through all the same routines. We have so few Christmases together, don't you see? I don't want to hide behind wrapping paper and M & M cookies. I was hoping we could put away all the decorations and just have us for a change.

LORNA: If I didn't know you better, I'd say you *planned* all this! Ralph? You didn't! You are out of your mind.

RALPH: I did not plan the "no vacancies"! I wouldn't have minded a few hours of sleep.

DANA: I don't believe you! Mike was supposed to call me tonight!

KYLE: And I was going to a Christmas party with Lauren!

LORNA: I had a ton of baking planned!

RALPH: Well, we're stuck together. Isn't that awful. I don't know, I sort of like being' around all of you on Christmas Eve. Wow! You know, it just hit me. I suddenly remember what it was I didn't have at Christmas. It wasn't a Christmas tree. No, no, no. We had that. And decorations. And presents. It was a *family* I didn't have! Now, of course, I didn't really have a family the rest of the year, either, but when a family is falling apart on Christmas, it just sort of hurts a little more. Doesn't it?

LORNA (*quietly*): Yes, it does.

KYLE: Whoa, Dad.

DANA: You never told us that before.

WAITRESS (comes in carrying menus): These are the breakfast menus. I'm going off shift now. Mark'll be your waiter.

RALPH: Can't wait to get home to those presents, huh?

WAITRESS: Ah, no, not really. I . . . ah, see I just moved here and . . . I don't really know anybody. My family's kinda far away. You don't want to hear this. Anyway, that's Mark over there. Merry Christmas, folks.

(WAITRESS goes out. Long pause. DANA stands up.)

LORNA: Where you going, honey?

DANA: I was . . . going to invite her to have breakfast with us. Is that okay? Dad? I mean, she said her family's far away. I know I sure wouldn't want to be far away from my family on Christmas. (She starts to go, but turns around.) Kyle, touch my hot chocolate and die.

(The lights fade to:

(Blackout.)

New Year's Re: Solution

A Monologue for New Year's

Cast

NANCY: a woman in her 30s to 50s

Scene

A kitchen

Props

Chair

Table

Wind-up clock

Yellow pad

Day Runner calendar book

Confetti

Chocolate bar

Costume

Modern

Running Time

4 minutes

Production Notes

Nancy has been through all the New Year's resolutions—more exercise, eating right, losing weight. This year, however, she's decided to eschew the worldly goals for something a little more heavenly-minded. By this time next year, Nancy has decided she's going to be a vibrantly spiritual woman of God.

And she can do it too. She's got a plan. She's got a program. And she'll do it. Even if it kills her.

"New Year's Re: Solution" is a humorous monologue on how we regiment spiritual change without allowing God to be part of the process. It dispels the "bootstrap" belief that we can do anything if we put ourselves on the right program and keep a stiff upper lip.

The monologue obviously goes over the top, so don't be afraid to play it that way. The alarm clock ringing at the right moment can be achieved by setting it to ring ahead of time and pulling out the alarm set tab when the actor picks it up.

This sketch can be performed the Sunday before New Year's or during a special church New Year's Eve program.

(Lights. A kitchen. NANCY *has a Day Runner calendar book open and is working on a yellow pad. A wind-up clock and a small pile of confetti set in front of her.)*

NANCY: Okay, five minutes till midnight. I can do this. This should be easy. All I have to do is figure out exactly what's wrong with my life and then come up with some kind of New Year's resolution to fix it. *(Thinks a moment.)* I don't know. All that's coming to mind is what's wrong with everybody else's lives and what they could do to fix theirs.

(Small pause.)

This year I want to make a real life-changing resolution. One that I can hold my head up about when I tell people. I've been through all the usual ones. Five years ago I swore I was going to lose 10 pounds that year. And I did. Of course, I didn't eat anything but candy canes and water from December 26 to January 1, but I did it. Four years ago, I decided I was going to exercise. I had a whole regimen set up—running, tennis, ironman triathlon. It was incredible. And I actually shaped up . . . running up and down the stairs in the mall looking for the right shoes, the rackets, the sweats, the Gatorade, the vitamins. I think I got a little upper arm tone putting all the stuff away on the top shelf of the storage closet. Two years ago my New Year's resolution was to start eating better. Reduce my cholesterol intake. Watch my triglycerides. Clean my body of all toxins. I bought spirulina, bee pollen, carrot juice, sargasso water. I subscribed to *Longevity* and *Whole Earth Times.* I took vitamin pills that would make a horse shudder. I ate pure for three weeks straight. Then one day in the checkout line over at the Healthnut I read a *Reader's Digest* article called, "The Chocolate Diet: Go Ahead, Make My Day." Well, I don't have to tell you . . . *(Takes a bite of a candy bar. Smiles.)* Now, last year my resolution was to have a really great resolution by midnight on the next New Year's. I've got three minutes.

(A beat. She sighs.)

Let me think. Where does my life really stink? That *is* a tough one. I don't know, this one might require a little prayer to figure . . . wait a minute.

Prayer! Of course! I've been saying for years that my spiritual life was going straight to . . . the dogs. This is perfect. All right, I've got it. My New Year's Resolution. *(An announcement.)* This year I'm going to get my spiritual life completely under control! I'll become a new person! I'll become a godly woman! I'll make sure of it. I'll come up with a program that can't fail. Wait till I tell the Women's Prayer Breakfast. They're still making carnal resolutions like not eating too many danish at the meetings. They'll be green when I tell them mine! Okay, I need a goal. I need a plan. I need a program. I'll . . . start with Bible study. Yeah. Okay, let's see.

(Opens her Day Runner. A deep sigh.)

I've got so much going here, I don't know when I'll be able to . . . That's it. I'll just get up at 4 A.M. I can have Bible study from 4 A.M. to 9:17 A.M. That'll give me over five hours of Bible study a day! That should do the trick. But that *will* only give me five hours of sleep. Okay, so I suffer a little. It's good for me. No pain, no . . . Oh, no, I forgot. I won't be able to drive Mrs. Schnauzer to her women's group on Tuesday and Thursday mornings. Ahhh, she can take the bus. She's only 83. I'll just tell her I'm doing something for God. That'll keep her from whining. Okay, then I'll pray every day from 10 A.M. to 12:43, and from 3:11 P.M. to 5:26. I'll make up a color spread sheet prayer list on the computer. And I can cross reference it with past requests, answers to prayer, and the requester's spiritual history.

(She writes a moment.)

Oh, I'm so excited! Okay, next I'll . . . subscribe to *Christianity Today, Christian Herald,* and *Saltshaker* magazines. Maybe a few more. I'll clip articles every morning after Bible study. And I'll read the collected works of Oswald Chambers, James Dobson, and Robert Schuler at night. I'll make notes on the laptop. I'll . . . buy a Walkman and listen to Scripture tapes while I exercise! *(Looks at her Day Runner.)* Oh, I won't have time to exercise with my new schedule. I'll have to quit going on visitation ministry too. Don't have time for it. And I'll have to get out of choir, cut back my hours at work, and stop helping my mother with her shopping. It'll all have to go! But it doesn't matter. I'll sacrifice whatever I have to to make myself a new person! I'll make a spread sheet of my new schedule and put it up on the refrigerator. I'll also put one in my Day Runner, in my car, in my Bible, and on the bathroom mirror! By this time next year, I'm going to be a vibrant, healthy, incredibly spiritual . . . WOMAN OF GOD! *(A beat.)* Even if it kills me.

(She holds up the clock.)

Five . . . four . . . three . . . two . . . ONE!

(The alarm goes off. NANCY *throws a handful of confetti into the air.)*

HAAAPPY NEEEW YEEEEAAAR!!

(Blackout.)

Bernie Clenchfist

A Monologue for Palm Sunday

Cast

BERNIE (OR BERNADETTE) CLENCHFIST: a nerd of any age

Scene

Curb on a parade roadside

Props

Two chairs	Ice chest
Newspaper	Fresca
Rock	Cheese puffs
Blanket	Doritos

Costume

Nerd outfit—high-waist slacks, taped glasses, baseball cap, etc.

Production Notes

It's the Palm Sunday parade, and Bernie Clenchfist thinks he can bring a rock to do his praising for him. True, Jesus said the rocks and stones would start to shout if we wouldn't, but when Bernie is face-to-face with his triumphant Savior, there's no other choice but to lift his hands.

This monologue is meant to augment a Palm Sunday service. It's a short piece, moving from the comedy of an outrageous character to the sincere worship of a believer.

Bernie, who can be played by either a man or a woman, by the way, is a classic nerd. You can be as crazy as you want with the costumes and the quirks. When we mounted the sketch, we gave him an outrageous Midwestern accent and filled the monologue with slobby bits. It really works in building toward the moment of connection with Jesus.

You can perform the sketch with or without the taped crowd noises. The rock should be of substantial size.

(The sound of a crowd. Lights. Two chairs. In one sits BERNIE CLENCHFIST, *a nerd in Hagar slacks, baseball cap, and taped glasses. In his back pocket is a rolled up newspaper. He has a blanket over his legs, an ice chest at his feet, an open can of Fresca with a straw, and an open bag of cheese puffs. In the other chair sits a rock.* BERNIE *has his ear pressed against the rock, listening intently.)*

BERNIE: I . . . I think I hear . . . I'm sure I hear this . . . I dunno . . . like a buzzing or something. Yeah, I hear this like . . . buzzing sound. I definitely hear it now. It's clear as all get out now. This buzzing! I think it's starting! I think it's happening! A . . . buzzing! Look out! Stand back! Buzz, buzz, bu . . .

(He pulls his face away. Sees it's a bug. He frowns and smashes it with the newspaper. He flicks it away.)

Shucks. I was so close. Thought I had somethin' there. *(Amazed.)* Well, you don't expect *me* to get all into it, do ya? Come on! It's just not part'a my nature, that's all. Getting all emotional and all. Okay, wait, I'll explain it to ya.

(He holds up the newspaper.)

Look, it says in here that Jesus is comin' by here today. Gonna walk right past here yet. Right here. I gotta spot right by the curb. Right in front, too, yet. I camped out for three days to get this spot. The chair, the blanket, the ice chest, the diet Fresca, the cheese puffs. Everything I need. The whole shebang.

(Looks at someone.)

Hey, pal, move it over! This is my spot. Yeah, both chairs! Sheesh! Look, my space is from there to there to there, got it? For your information, the rock is holding the chair down, okay?

(Winks at the audience.)

That always gets 'em ta shuddup. Anyways, I'm not the parade type, normally. Y'know, all those people showin' up in their RVs from Kansas and all to see some stupid float. I personally do not get into it, okay? People screamin' at some 30-foot high mammal made outta petunias or somethin'. But this is Jesus we're talking about, and I figured, it's history here. It's the thing to do. But I am *not* gonna get up and start shoutin' and praisin' like most'a these people around here are gonna be doin'. You know what I mean? Now, I'm as excited about God and Jesus and stuff as the next guy, y'know. It's just that I refuse to wave my hands in the air and look like a first-class yahoo in full bloom. Nuh-uh. This is the way I figure it. Last time through Jesus said the stones would start to praise if everybody clammed up. So I brought Rocky along here to make a little test'a the theory.

(He looks at the rock. A beat.)

So. You gonna just sit there like a lump, are ya? *(Leans in.)* Look, I bought ya a whole bag'a Doritos! What more d'ya want? All I can tell ya is, ya better not make me look like a—

(Sound of a crowd, building. BERNIE *looks up.)*

What? He's comin' this way? Where? Over there! Yeah, I see 'im! *(Smacks the rock.)* Okay, Rocky, it's showtime, pal. Do yer stuff. Can't ya see 'im? Over there! Look, I'm waitin'!

(Turns Rocky's chair to give him a better vista.)

Look, look! All right . . . praise! Come on, get into it. Sing! Shout! Come on! Don't make me do this by myself! *(Looks up.)* Hey, quit crowdin' me here! Hey, people, move back, I can't see a blessed thing! Get outta the way!

(He stands.)

Incredible! He's right there! Move over . . . get back, I can't see! *(Calls.)* Hey, Jesus! Over here! *(Looks at Rocky.)* Just great! I gotta get a rock with stage fright!

(Gets up on the chair.)

Hey, over here! Jesus! It's Bernie. *(Gingerly raises one hand to the shoulder, slightly waving.)* Over here! Can you see me? Yo, Jesus! Look over here! *(Raises his hand higher, beginning to wave frantically.)* Yeah, look over here! It's Bernie! Look at me! Look at—!

*(*BERNIE *freezes, wide-eyed for a moment. He looks down at Rocky.)*

He sees me! He's lookin' at me! HE KNOWS ME! *(The other hand starts coming up, waving.)* Yeah! It's me! Bernie! Praise . . . praise You . . . praise You, Jesus! He knows me! Bless You, Jesus! PRAISE YOU!

(Both hands fully up, outstretched in adoration.)

HALLELUJAH!!

(Blackout.)

Three O'clock

A Monologue for Good Friday

Cast

ACTOR: a man or woman of any age

Props

Stool

Costume

Modern. Dark clothes. (Biblical is an option.)

Running Time

2 minutes

Production Time

"Three O'clock" is a simple monologue written out in verse form. It delves into the idea that Jesus died of a broken heart, His cardiac sac rupturing against the pressure of the sacrifice. Hence, the blood and water.

This can be read or memorized—although working without a script is preferable. This is not a piece to be rushed. Each stanza is designed to be a vignette. Take your time.

(Lights. An actor on a tall stool. Gradually, the diffused stage light pulls in until there is only a spot on the actor.)

ACTOR: It is three o'clock.

    The sky roils black, thunder groans across the valley.
    In three hours the Sabbath will begin.

    It is three o'clock.
    A bleary bartender twists away from a prattling regular. Notices the sky.
    Is startled. Only for a moment. He turns back to the wine and the buzzing brains.

    It is three o'clock.

    Quick! The soldiers break the legs of the two lingering thieves.
    They smash their bones with fist-thick clubs.

    It is three o'clock.

    On a dark-sudden day. A dismayed mother whistles in her children.
    Unable to give reason to the swollen, screaming sky.

    It is three o'clock.

    The Nazarene sags into His agony.
    Betrayed, beaten, battered to a cross.
    His heart is brim full—
    Bulging.
    Ponderous.
    Pressure crushes pressure . . .
    Gasping . . .
    Trembling.

    Stuffed in His frame the countless rock-hard
    hearts . . . crack . . .
    cracking open . . .
    His . . .
    It cannot withstand the weight of . . .

    It is three o'clock.

    The sun is eclipsed.
    The earth is shaken.
    And Jesus of Nazareth has died
    of a broken heart.

(Blackout.)

Easter Unawares

A Sketch for Easter

Cast

GLEN: a man in his 30s to 40s
LAURIE: a woman in her 30s to 40s
MAN: a man of whatever age

Scene

A front room

Props

Chair	Dyed Easter eggs
Coffee table	Basket
TV	Coffee cup
Remote	Spoon
TV Guide	

Costumes

Modern

Running Time

12 minutes

Production Notes

A disciple, an angel, a lunatic, or just a dream? Something happened to Glen on Easter while his wife and kids were at a sunrise service. Something that reminded him an empty tomb is the most incredible event of all time.

"Easter Unawares" is a "Twilight Zone"-like sketch following the early-morning story of a man who has a strange visitor and is vividly reminded of what a faith in the Resurrection is all about.

The front room can be as detailed or sparse as you want to make it. Doors and windows can be pantomimed. It's best to have a working TV with the sound turned way down.

Don't play MAN as otherworldly. The audience needs to wonder if he's for real throughout the sketch.

(*Lights. Dawn. Shadowy. A front room. The lights in the front room are off. After a moment, a shadowed figure comes into the room. It hits its toe on a piece of furniture and shouts, then mumbles under its breath.*)

LAURIE (*off*): Glen? Glen is that—?

GLEN (*barking*): Me? Of course it's me!

LAURIE: Are you—?

GLEN: Up? Who could sleep! You're making enough noise to wake the—

LAURIE (*off*): So, are you—?

GLEN: Going? No, I am not going! (*He finally manages to switch on the light. He blinks, wearily. He's dressed in a bathrobe, carries a blanket and a coffee cup with a spoon still in it. He limps to his chair.*) I already told you that. I said it lying down; I'll say it standing up. (*He sits.*) I am not—!

LAURIE (*off*): I made coffee.

GLEN: I know! Want to know how I know? (*Rattles the spoon around in his cup.*) D'you hear that, Laurie? Can you hear that tink, tink, tinking? That's how I know there's coffee. Who could sleep with five pounds of Cremora, a box of Equal, and your spoon of death!

LAURIE (*off*): What?

(*He sighs. Drinks his coffee. LAURIE comes in, dressed in her Sunday best and fastening an earring.*)

LAURIE: Oh, you're in here.

GLEN: In body only. Do you know it's not even 6 A.M. yet?

LAURIE: Couldn't sleep, huh, Glen? Guilt, maybe?

GLEN: I can sleep with guilt, Laurie. (*Picks up the spoon.*) It's this I can't sleep with.

96

LAURIE (*calling off*): Jordan! Jamie! Both of you grab your heavy jackets. (*To* GLEN.) So, you're up, why don't you come with us to the service?

GLEN: I already told you I'm not going.

LAURIE: It'll only take you a few minutes to throw something on.

GLEN: Throw something on? Excuse me, but isn't this Easter morning service we're talking about? You think I can just throw on any old rag? That'd be sacrilegious, wouldn't it? I mean, with everyone dressed to the nines for their little brunch appearances.

LAURIE: That's not how it is.

GLEN: No? Didn't you know Peter and John had on three-piece suits when they ran to the tomb?

LAURIE: Glen, nobody cares what you're dressed like.

GLEN: Naïveté, thy name is Laurie. C'mon, I grew up in church. I know what it's like on Easter morning.

LAURIE: Well, maybe a few things have changed since 1959.

GLEN: That's not one of 'em.

LAURIE (*off*): No coloring books, Jamie! We're going to church. *Church.* Go on out to the car. (*To* GLEN.) Come on. Change your mind. It'd be a nice way to start the holiday. A sunrise service.

GLEN: I've got fistfuls of fake grass, foot-high chocolate bunnies, and a furry friend coming to visit in just a little while. What do I need with 10 hymns, a 45-minute sermon, and cold metal chairs?

LAURIE: I don't know why I let you get to me.

GLEN (*holds up "TV Guide"*): The "Holy Book" says there are 11 million Easter programs on this morning. Plenty to keep me from backsliding until you get home.

LAURIE: You know, last Easter it was the same routine. You got up at the crack of dawn with the rest of us, then sat there and took potshots at my enthusiasm.

GLEN: Look, you and I don't go the rest of the year. I'm not going to be a hypocrite and make a cameo appearance on Easter.

LAURIE: Well, I'll take the risk, thank you very much.

GLEN: God's all-powerful, isn't He? He can hear me at home.

LAURIE: What makes you so sure there'll be anything worth listening to?

GLEN: Oh, and who's taking potshots now? Come on. The celebration's not off just because one person doesn't make it to the party.

LAURIE: No. But the party's not the same, either. I have to go. Make sure you hide the eggs this time before we get home. I don't want to find you asleep in front of the TV like last year.

GLEN *(trying to hug her):* Laurie, come on—

LAURIE: The kids are in the car.

GLEN *(suddenly):* I am not going to let you make me feel guilty because I can't get excited about all this anymore! And I am not going to sit around in a coat and tie and pretend I'm interested.

LAURIE: You're telling me you don't believe anymore?

GLEN: No. I'm telling you I just don't care.

LAURIE: What's the difference?

(They look at each other for a moment. She goes out.)

GLEN *(calling after her):* Make sure to tell pastor I'm home with the flu! I'll have the eggs hidden. I promise.

(A door slams off.)

No, I don't want to go to the Christmas cantata! No, I don't want to go to the church banquet! No, I don't want to go to the sunrise service! STOP ASKING ME! It's like a bad marriage. No desire left, but you're still supposed to go through the motions.

(He remotes on the TV.)

Lessee if I can find one who ain't askin' for money. *(Flips through the stations.)* This is perfect! I can get one with robes and one without. *(Flips.)* And this guy! Oh, he looks too perfect. They must have lowered that hair on him with a crane. *(Flips.)* Uh-oh. Dr. White-Hair. Ooooo, that mean look supposed to scare me? Yikes, where's my checkbook. *(Flips.)* And here he is. Every year since they invented Easter. Man, he's looking old. Makeup's not even working anymore. *(Flips.)* Here we are. This is the one I wanted. Rev. Road Runner and Pastor Wile E. Coyote.

(He puts down the remote and pulls the blanket up. After a moment, he nods off. Jerks his head up. He looks at the TV. Laughs. Nods off again. He nods and wakes several times until he finally drops off. Pause. A knock at the door. Another knock, louder, more insistent. A beat. GLEN sits up. He looks at the TV, disoriented. Now a pounding at the door.)

GLEN *(looking at his watch, blinking):* Oh, no! *(Flips off the TV and calls off.)* Just a minute, Laurie! Great. . . . I did it again. Where are the—?

(He bolts off and comes back in with a basket of dyed Easter eggs. Another knock. Loud.)

I'm on my way! Come on, give me a minute, will you! Why'd you make so many of these. There must be a million. Okay . . . I'd better put some of them in the bedrooms and . . . then the backyard. *(He runs off.)* I unlocked the door for you, hon! Be right there!

(A door slams, off. A beat. MAN *strides into the room, looking excited, out of breath—and a little wary. He's dressed in old, worn clothes and has a scruffy beard—but he does not look like a street person. He looks around a moment. He goes to the "window" and cautiously looks out. Then he smiles and pulls open the blind. Sunlight streams in.* GLEN *breezes through the front room on his way to the kitchen.)*

GLEN: Cryin' out loud, honey! You couldn't tell I was trying to stall you? (GLEN *goes out. A beat. He dashes back in and sees* MAN *at the window. He drops his basket of eggs.)* How'd you get in here?!

MAN: Don't worry. It's all right now. See, I can even open the window.

GLEN: I'm an idiot! I just unlocked the door for him! *(Moves toward* MAN *cautiously.)* Go away. You hear me? You can't just walk into people's homes! Get out! You want me to call the police?

MAN *(coming toward him):* Hey, hey. Don't be afraid. It's me.

GLEN: All right, all right! What do you want? Food? Is that it? I've got some eggs right here. *(Hands him some dyed eggs, which* MAN *looks at curiously.)* Go for it. That's good protein there. Okay, a little high on the cholesterol. What's your problem? They're not rotten, buddy. They're dyed. What d'you expect when you come looking for a handout on Easter morning!

MAN: Easter? Look, we ain't got time to eat now. The whole city's gonna be in an uproar. We gotta hurry!

GLEN: What are you talking about?

MAN: Come on, I'll tell you about it on the way. None of us knows what's gonna happen next. There might be some trouble, so we should all be together. Why are you just standing there? I ran all the way over here to get you. You should know how dangerous that is.

GLEN: Dangerous?

MAN: C'mon, I'll tell you all about it. We'll take one'a the side streets. We're still a little afraid of the priests.

GLEN: Well, I wouldn't know anything about that. I'm a Presbyterian.

MAN: A what?

GLEN: A Presbyterian. Look, buddy, I'm in a real hurry at the moment, so why don't you just spit it out.

MAN (confused by GLEN's attitude; leans closer): You're never gonna believe what happened.

GLEN: Try me.

MAN: What I'm gonna tell you is the most fantastic thing you're ever gonna hear. In your whole life.

GLEN: I'm all ears.

MAN: It's about . . . the tomb.

GLEN: The tomb?

MAN: Where they buried Him. You remember.

GLEN (catching on): You mean . . . Jesus.

MAN: Of course!

GLEN: Great! A religious nut! I don't go to church, so they gotta come to me!

MAN: I'm not a nut! I know it's hard to believe, but I thought you'd want to be the first to know. Early in the morning some'a the women went over to the tomb, and you know what they found?

GLEN: A shot in the dark here: The tomb was empty.

MAN (reeling back): WHO TOLD YOU?!

GLEN: What do you mean, who told me?

MAN: Only a few of us know. We only just found out.

GLEN: What rock you been hiding under?

MAN: I'll admit it. We've been hiding. We were afraid. But you! You know?! How come you're not over with the rest of us celebrating and worshiping?!

GLEN: Ah . . . I've been busy.

MAN: You were coming over later?

GLEN: Yeah. I always like going later. The . . . pastor's warmed up by then. In fact, I was just looking for my Sunday best—

MAN: It don't matter! Nothin' matters now! I've been bawlin' my eyes out all morning! Who would'a guessed this? It answers everything, don't it?

GLEN: Well, not everything.

MAN: We were so stupid to doubt Him. I can see that now.

GLEN (enjoying the game): I hate to tell you this, pal, but I never doubted Him. Not for a second.

MAN: You mean you knew? All along?

GLEN: He had it planned from the beginning. Dropped hints right and left, for cryin' out loud. Don't you remember, "For just as Jonah was in the belly of the sea monster for three days—"

MAN: "So, the Son'a Man will be in the heart of the earth!" You're right! I never put that together.

GLEN: Those disciples were such idiots. I can't believe they couldn't figure it out.

MAN *(hurt):* Oh . . . Well, you know, you always did have a strong faith.

GLEN: What kind of crack was that?

MAN: If there's ever gonna be someone who could never lose faith, it's you.

GLEN *(furious):* All right, who sent you?

MAN: What?

GLEN: Somebody from the church sent you over here! Is this some kind of bizarre campaign to bring in the lost sheep?

MAN: I just thought you'd wanna be with us!

GLEN *(grabs* MAN's *arm):* Well, thanks for the offer. Sorry you had to come all this way.

MAN: Why're you sorry! The tomb is empty! It's the most incredible thing that's ever happened!

GLEN: Sure, sure. Easter's great.

MAN: Easter? Look, don't you wanna come back with me?

GLEN: No, thanks. You have a good time, though.

MAN: Okay, but you be careful. We don't know what'll happen when the town hears about it.

GLEN: The town? Look, half the town's sleeping in today, and the other half's dusting off their yellow bonnets and hoping the sermon doesn't run too late.

MAN: What are you talking about?

GLEN: What am I—? I've had enough of this! Tell me what you want and get out of here!

MAN: What I want? Didn't you hear me? The tomb's empty.

GLEN: Okay. *(A beat.)* That's it? No tracts or anything?

MAN: What's the matter with you? You act like nothing's happened.

GLEN: It's old news, pal. OLD NEWS! I hate to rain on your delusions, but everybody knows already.

MAN (stunned): How . . . how can everybody know? It just happened two hours ago!

GLEN (after a beat): Two hours ago?

MAN: Yeah, at sunrise.

GLEN (under): Have we got a live one here . . .

MAN: What's happened to you? You act like you don't even care. He used to be your whole life!

GLEN: Now, that's none of your—

MAN: Every word He said used to—

GLEN: SHUT UP! Okay, your game just ended, buddy. You can just go tell whoever sent you that I am not interested, okay?

MAN (floored): Not interested?

GLEN: NOT INTERESTED!!

MAN: You're not the same. Who are you? Is it because you're afraid?

GLEN: I am not going to discuss my spiritual status with a shopping-cart schizo! For your information, I am not afraid of anything! I JUST GOT TIRED OF ONE-SIDED CONVERSATIONS! And the last thing I need is for some lunatic to come in here and spoon-feed me guilt trips on Easter morning!

MAN: Easter?

GLEN: Easter, Easter! Christmas, New Year's, Valentine's Day, St. Patrick's Day, EASTER! Quit jerking me around! Some religious group sent you over here. So, you got a magazine you want me to buy now, is that it? JUST TELL ME WHAT YOU WANT?!

(Pause.)

MAN: I want to tell you He's alive.

(MAN looks at GLEN for a long moment, then puts the eggs down on the coffee table. He goes out.)

GLEN (calling after him): Why don't you hit Sinclair's house next door! He ain't been in church since Billy Graham preached in a tent! (Paces.) I can't believe this! Some loony breaks into my house and wants to know what's wrong with me? Last thing I need is some fanatic blabbing about an empty tomb on Easter. *(Shakes it off.)* That was spooky. He floats in here like he's from . . . another world or something, and tries to tell me that . . . *(He looks off.)* . . . Jesus!

(GLEN dashes off. A moment later, the door slams and he dashes in, breathless.)

Oh, I knew it! It's too perfect! I run outside and there's no trace of 'im! Anywhere! It's too classic! *(A deep breath.)* Okay, don't be an idiot. He probably high-tailed it around the corner. Thought I'd call the police. Maybe he really went to Sinclair's place. Naw.

(He pounces on the phone and dials.)

Come on, Harry. I know you're home. You wouldn't be caught dead going to . . . Hello? Harry? Ah, howdy, neighbor. Listen, just a quick question here—yeah, I know it's early. I know it's Sunday morning. Harry, just one . . . listen, Harry, you got some kind of . . . street person around your place? All right, a bum. You got a bum in your bushes or something? Nobody pounded on your front door talking about the empty tomb? Empty tomb, Harry. You know, Jesus-rose-from-the-dead stuff? Harry? Harry? *(Slams the phone down.)* The pagan. *(Picks up the Easter egg basket.)* All right. I'm not going to jump to any conclusions. I'm just going to make like Peter Cottontail and forget the whole thing. Okay. The . . . ah, backyard. I'll hide these in the backyard.

(He goes out. A moment later, LAURIE comes in.)

LAURIE: Oh, Flopsy? You through with the you-know-what? *(Looks around.)* Glen? The kids are still in the car. You finished yet? *(Sees the eggs on the coffee table.)* Well, you could have tried a little harder than this.

(GLEN suddenly bolts in and sees LAURIE. He shouts and drops the basket. LAURIE also jumps.)

Are you out of your mind?!

GLEN: You see anybody out front? Walking down the street? A . . . a street person . . . a bum . . . an angel?

LAURIE: No, I didn't. All I saw was Harry Sinclair stomping around in his bushes. What's going on?

GLEN: I don't know . . .

LAURIE: Oh, Glen! We had a prowler, didn't we? I'd better get the kids!

GLEN: It wasn't a prowler. It was . . . just some guy wanted to tell me something . . . ah, wanted something to eat.

LAURIE: Well, I hope you chased him off!

GLEN *(sits, lost in thought):* I did.

LAURIE: I'm glad the kids weren't here. Glen? Are you all right? You want me to call the police? Glen? Glen, did he try and hurt you?

GLEN (*quietly*): No.

(GLEN *picks up the Easter eggs. He looks at them, then begins cracking the eggs and peeling off the colored shells.*)

LAURIE: Well, it's over now, Hon. We can enjoy the rest of the day, can't we? (*Calls off.*) Kids, come on! (*Takes off her coat and gloves.*) It was such a nice service. It always makes me feel so good when I go. You should have been there. The choir sounded better than last year. They had a whole batch of that Easter bread. You know, the loaves with whole eggs cooked right in the middle. And everybody looked so nice. You really missed something.

(*Small pause. She walks to* GLEN.)

Glen? You all right, honey? (*Getting a little frightened.*) Honey, did that bum say something to you? Something to upset you? Come on, Glen. Forget about it. Let's look for the eggs, now, huh? It's Easter. Honey, don't let that man ruin your day.

(LAURIE *lets the blinds fall. The lights go to:*

(*Blackout.*)

Up from the Grave He Arose

A Teen Sketch for Easter

Cast

AUSTIN
MARK
DANA
AMY
KURT
All teenagers

Scene

A city park. Just before sunrise.

Props

Chairs

Costumes

Sweats, jeans, jackets, etc.

Running Time

7 minutes

Production Notes

What is our proof that Jesus rose from the dead? It's the fact the life has been infused into death for 2,000 years. The Resurrection is being poured into believers with the same power as it was in Jerusalem, A.D. 33.

That's the point of "Up from the Grave He Arose." Teenagers setting up chairs for a sunrise service realize that Jesus is alive because their hearts—and in some cases, their bodies—are.

Have a few chairs in the beginning to give the feeling of rows. Make sure the actors are really bringing in chairs and setting them up as they talk. And, as in other sketches with slang, let the actors change the vernacular to what they feel comfortable with.

There are light cues in the script, but if you don't have anything special, don't worry about it.

(Lights. A city park. Just before sunrise. Folding chairs in rows. More chairs stacked to side or on a trolley. AUSTIN is sprawled over a chair, dead asleep. He's snoring louder than a Metallica concert. MARK, DANA, AMY, and KURT come in, all carrying folding chairs, talking and laughing. MARK signals for them to be quiet. He creeps over to AUSTIN.)

MARK (opera voice): "Up from the Grave He Aroooooooose!"

(AUSTIN freaks. Tries to stand but falls over his chair.)

AUSTIN: Wha . . . what's happening?!

MARK: What's happening is you *not* helping us, bone.

AUSTIN (stands, blows on his frozen hands): So, this is what dawn looks like, huh. This happen every morning? (Starts setting up some chairs.) Man, who invented sunrise services, anyway? It's colder 'n my vice principal's heart out here.

AMY: Nobody invented it. That's when the Resurrection happened, doof.

AUSTIN: Why couldn't they have picked a better time? Like, July . . . about noon.

MARK: Then you'd be complaining about how hot it was.

KURT: Shag it, Austin. People'll be starting to show up here in about a half hour.

DANA: You guys ever notice how we *always* get the zero-brain jobs?

(They all groan in agreement. AUSTIN sits.)

You know? They ask the youth group to come to the church banquet. Do we getta cook the steaks and serve the wilty lettuce? No. We getta wash dishes. They ask us to come down and help on Spruce Up the Church Saturday. Do we getta drive the lawn mower and work the leaf blower. No. We getta rake leaves and clean the toilets.

AMY: I know. When they asked us to help with the church sunrise service, I'm all "Great! We're going to sing or give our testimonies or somethin'." But what do we getta do?

KURT/AMY/DANA/MARK: Set up chairs.

(AUSTIN *snores. They all look at him.* KURT *goes to him and clangs metal chairs together.*)

AUSTIN *(bolting up):* Agggghhhh! This is crazy! What're we doing? God's not even awake yet! These people are gonna be singing and stuff out here, and God's all, "Hey! At least wait'll my alarm goes off!"

AMY: Well, your alarm just went off, pal. Grab some'a those chairs.

(They continue setting chairs up in rows.)

KURT: I might be bizarre, but do any of the rest of you even feel like its Easter?

MARK: You're right. You're bizarre.

KURT: Come on, y'know what I mean. You guys feel like it's some kinda special day? A . . . I don't know, a holy day or something? Any of you? Me neither. I mean, not right now, anyway. I'm getting dressed to come down here and all I'm thinking about is how it doesn't feel like Easter. And now it's almost over.

AMY: I know. It's like, you always know it's Christmas. You'd have to be the geek of the Universe to not know it's Christmas. But Easter? It can slip right past you.

AUSTIN: What're you talking about? I don't know about the rest'a you, but I've got a solid milk-chocolate duck the size of Texas back at my house. I'm gonna have a sugar buzz that'll take me to graduation. *I* sure know it's Easter.

DANA: When I was younger, we *always* knew it was Easter around my house. We used to have these phenomenal Easter egg hunts, you know? Then my dad went and had his stupid cholesterol checked. Happy Scrambler tofu eggs are not the same thing.

MARK: Well, my parents don't even know what Easter is. They call it "Rebirth-day" or something. I don't know. I had to put a crystal on and tell 'em I was going to the "Spring's Awakening Harmonic Regeneration Maypole Dance and Yogafest" just to get to come down here. *(He adopts a lotus position and "Ommm.")*

AMY: Easter's weird. I mean, you can't pretend you're all into Easter, you know? I don't know. It's like . . . I mean, with Christmas, you know, if you don't feel the whole Bethlehem thing, you can still join the party. Sing a couple of carols, open some presents, drive around and look at all the beautiful lights and stuff. But not Easter. Easter's serioso. It's not shepherds and "Silent Night" and little babies with no crying they make. Easter's this . . . holiday about a torn-up guy walking out of a hole in the ground and promising everyone they're never going to die. I mean, I guess it's still a party, but you can't put your mind on autopilot or something and just join in the fun.

DANA *(after a moment):* Never thought of it that way before.

MARK: I talk to my parents until I pop a vein about the Resurrection and stuff. And they're all, "Easter is a celebration of rebirth." "Jesus is just a symbol of spring's new life." And I wanna shout at 'em, "Jesus is not the *symbol* of new life, He IS new life!" Someone walking out of a grave. You know, people can't deal, so they make 'im a symbol.

KURT: Can you blame people? Somebody coming back from the dead? That's scary. If you don't believe it, how you gonna explain it? If I wasn't a Christian, I'd call Jesus just a symbol too. 'Cuz if you *are* gonna believe it, your whole life's gonna wake up.

(AUSTIN *cuts loose with a huge snore.*)

DANA: I can't believe him.

AMY *(over* AUSTIN, *D.I. delivery):* MOVE IT, PRIVATE DORK!

AUSTIN *(straight up):* Come on, Mom! My first class ain't until 8:30! *(Sees them.)* Wasn't my mom just here?

KURT: Yeah. And she left a note. *(Pretends to read it.)* "Please excuse Little Austie from setting up chairs today. He's been lame all week."

AUSTIN *(heading off):* Great.

ALL: Leave and die.

AUSTIN: Just kidding.

AMY: Snap out of it, Austin. It's Easter.

AUSTIN: So.

MARK: Jesus walks out of a grave and you're still trying to crawl out of bed.

AUSTIN: I wish I was still in it.

AMY: Then why're you here?

AUSTIN: My mom made me come.

KURT: I'm devastated. You mean, you didn't *want* to come down here and help us celebrate Easter by banging chairs around in subzero weather?

AUSTIN: No way. I don't believe in Easter. My parents do. I'm just along for the ride. (*Makes the sound of a car horn, guns the motor.*) Get outta my way! Look ooouuut!

DANA: You're kidding me.

AUSTIN: Uh-uh. Far as I'm concerned, it was a big mistake. Jesus is still dead somewhere. Someone went to the wrong tomb; somebody stole the body; they all lied about seein' Him. Whatever. It just didn't happen.

AMY (*floored*): Get out.

AUSTIN: Hey. I can deal. (*He goes off to get chairs.*)

AMY: He's telling us Jesus is still dead?

MARK: I'll tell you something. If Jesus didn't rise from the dead, I'd'a burned my brains to a crisp by now. Vegetable paste. I didn't change because of death, dude, I changed 'cuz of life.

KURT: I heard that.

AMY: What Austin said, those're just . . . what do you call 'em? . . . cover-ups, right? Somebody made them all up.

DANA: Yeah, the disciples got all crucified or burned alive because Jesus DIDN'T rise from the dead. Millions of people have gotten cleaned up because Jesus DIDN'T rise from the dead. My dad hasn't had a drop of JD in 10 years because Jesus DIDN'T rise from the dead.

KURT: Don't you get it? Austin doesn't really mean Jesus is dead. Jesus is just dead for Austin.

(AUSTIN *walks in and sets up chairs. He sits down. A ray of sunlight hits his face.*)

AUSTIN: Hey, look, the sun's decided to show up.

AMY: That's great.

MARK: Look at that.

DANA: I've always felt like the sunrise was a little more beautiful on Easter morning.

(*They watch the sunrise for a moment.*)

AMY: Come on. We better get the rest of the chairs set up.

DANA: I guess so.

KURT: I don't know what it is, but right now, all'a sudden—

AMY: It finally feels like Easter, right?

KURT: Absolutely.

(*They walk off. *MARK* lags behind. He watches *AUSTIN* a moment, who has fallen dead asleep in the light.*)

MARK (*quietly*): I hope you wake up, Austin.

(*The lights go to:*

(*Blackout.*)

Power Walking

A Sketch for After Easter
Based on Luke 24:13-35

Cast

DEBBIE: a woman in her 20s to 50s
CLEO: her husband, a man in his 20s to 50s
JESUS: a man of whatever age

Scene

A road

Props

A road sign
Walkmans

Costumes

Sweat outfits

Running Time

4-5 minutes

Production Notes

In the middle of the flurry of the Resurrection victory, Jesus chooses to walk with two lonely disciples on the road to Emmaus.

That's what has always entranced us about the Emmaus Road story. Not that Jesus disappeared from their sight, but that He chose to be *in* their sight, out in the middle of nowhere, walking along their road.

"Power Walking," another Enscoe contempo-Scripture, takes up the faith journeys of Cleopas and his wife (here called Debbie—who knows why) and sets it squarely in the milieu of the '90s with Nike "Airs" and Walkmans. Debbie believes the Resurrection is the only answer to the Crucifixion. Cleo believes the Crucifixion leaves too many questions about a Resurrection.

Have fun with the road sign. You can add several arrows on the sign stand, EMMAUS, JERUSALEM, HELSINKI, BOISE. Jesus can be a man or a woman—your choice. Make sure Cleo and Debbie's outfits look chichi.

This sketch was designed for Easter Sunday night or for use within the first few weeks after Easter.

(Lights. Afternoon. A road. A traditional signpost with an arrow pointing to EMMAUS and to JERUSALEM. We hear heavy breathing. CLEO and DEBBIE, dressed in sweats and Walkmans, come up the aisle doing the swivel-hip, heel-toe power walk. They hit the playing area very out of breath.)

CLEO: Are . . . you hearing what I'm hearing?! Are you on the same station as me?

DEBBIE (pulling off her earphones, panting furiously): I—

CLEO (to her): What? (Listening.) Wait a minute! Did you hear that?! Did you hear what the newsguy just said?! The world has gone crazy!

DEBBIE: I . . . I—

CLEO (to her): Huh—? (Listening.) It's impossible! I can't believe they're reporting such bunk! I can't believe anyone is taking this seriously!

DEBBIE: I . . . be . . . be—

CLEO (to her): Speak up, I can't— (Listening.) WHAT?! Ridiculous! No way! I just don't—

DEBBIE: BELIEVE IT!

CLEO (pulling off his earphones): What did you say?

DEBBIE: I believe it. Every word. It's the only explanation.

CLEO: It is not the only explanation! It's only an explanation that's going to need more explanations!

DEBBIE (laughing, she starts to stretch out): It's so out of the blue. Who could have expected it?

CLEO: Out of the blue? It's out of this world! This is crazy! They said one of our own people told the story. Haven't we been laughed at enough as it is? And now this. The whole town's going to think we're all nutcakes.

DEBBIE: If it's true, Cleo, and we don't believe it, then we *are* nutcakes.

CLEO: I don't believe what I'm hearing! First He was an interesting guy, then He was a great public speaker, then came the Messiah routine—and now He has power over life and death?!

DEBBIE: Well, what about the appearances?

CLEO: What?

DEBBIE: That's what they said. They said there've been appearances. He's talked to several people already today.

CLEO: Appearances are deceiving! They . . . They're all hysterical. That's all there is to it. Everyone's too emotional about what's happened the last few days, and their minds're playing tricks on 'em.

DEBBIE *(trying to do a tough stretch):* Would you just exercise your mind a little and see the perfectness of it. See how it makes sense.

CLEO *(wincing):* I'd have to stretch over backwards for this to make sense. I'll tell you what makes sense. To stop trusting in anyone but yourself. *(Squeezes his skin.)* See this? This is a body. A real body. When it goes, I go. If you rely on someone else, when they go, you're still here trying to figure out what happened and how you're gonna go on with your life. No thank you. Now, hustle up, it's two miles to town yet. We need to keep the old shell in shape, huh? We've had enough things let us down lately. (CLEO *pops on his earphones, starts down an aisle.)*

DEBBIE: Would you hold on a minute!

CLEO *(talking a little louder because of the Walkman):* Just face it, Debbie! Any shmoe who goes around sayin' they've seen Jesus walkin' around now is either dead asleep and dreamin' or is one major candidate for the cuckoo bin.

(JESUS, *who has been sitting on an aisle seat, suddenly stands up in* CLEO's *path. He is dressed in a white jogger's suit with the hood pulled up.)*

Hey, one side or the other, buddy!

(CLEO *arcs around* JESUS *and continues on.* JESUS *looks up at* DEBBIE, *who is retying her shoe, Walkman earphones back in place.)*

JESUS: What was he talking about?

(Somehow, DEBBIE *has heard* JESUS. *She pulls off the earphones and looks at them. She shakes them. She checks the tape player. She sees* JESUS.)

DEBBIE: Did you just say something to me?

JESUS: What were you two talking about?

DEBBIE: You haven't heard what happened here over the weekend?

JESUS: I've been . . . out of town.

DEBBIE: You do know who Jesus is, don't you?

(JESUS *nods.*)

They killed Him and buried Him last Friday.

JESUS: And?

DEBBIE: And now people are saying He's risen from the dead. They say He's even going around talking to people.

CLEO *(from the aisle):* The only people who say they've seen Him are the kind that push shopping carts around and talk to themselves!

JESUS *(spinning to* CLEO): Didn't you *know* that He would have to suffer these things and then enter His glory?

CLEO: What? You have got to be from out of town!

JESUS: You could say that.

CLEO: So what do you know about it? "Enter His glory"? You ever seen a crucifixion, mister? There's nothing glorified about it. He was torn to shreds.

DEBBIE: What did you mean when you said, "Didn't you know He would have to suffer?"

JESUS: You know your scripture, don't you?

DEBBIE: Since we were kids. What good's it done us?

JESUS: Then you'll remember the prophecies. All the words about the Messiah who would come, suffer, and die.

CLEO: Hey, I went to Bible college, pal! I could give you half a dozen interpretations for all those passages.

JESUS *(to* DEBBIE): I'd love to talk with you about it. I'll walk with you. Which way are you heading?

DEBBIE *(points to Jerusalem):* That way. But we're kind of in a hurry right now.

CLEO: Yeah, we'll probably be moving too fast for you. What kind of shape are you in?

JESUS: Oh, I'll stay with you. Don't worry about that. I'm a lot stronger than you think.

(DEBBIE *nods. She takes off her Walkman and holds it in her hand. She starts off down the aisle.* JESUS *keeps pace with her. They pass* CLEO, *who watches them.*)

CLEO: What is it about that guy? *(Puts on his phones, starts to go, but stops. He takes a deep breath. Rubs his chest.)* Hoo, boy. I think I'm getting heartburn.

(Blackout.)

First Date

A Monologue for Mother's Day

Cast

BARRETT: a teenage boy

Scene

A front doorstep

Props

Flowers
A list
Potted plants (opt.)
A door frame (opt.)

Costume

Modern hip

Running Time

3-4 minutes

Production Notes

"The way you treat your mom is the way you'll treat your wife."

That's what Barrett's mom told him. And he's quickly finding out it's true. So Barrett is suddenly getting a crash course on how important his mother is to him—and how to survive the storms of a relationship by what she has taught him.

Part humorous observation, part confessional, "First Date" looks at a young man's discovery of the love and care of his mother.

Don't let on in the action that Barrett's "date" is really with his mother. It should have all the earmarks of a formal date with a girlfriend.

You can suggest the porch by potted plants in a square and a door frame. Or just a door frame.

Give the actor all the time he needs. Take your pauses to heart.

(Lights. A front porch. BARRETT *in his mid to late teens, is dressed up pretty nice. Hip, but nice. His hair is styled. He's holding a bunch of flowers. He looks a bit nervous. This has all the earmarks of a first date.)*

BARRETT: I'm real new at this kind of thing, I gotta tell ya. This . . . I don't know . . . this formal kind of thing with flowers and all. I'm wondering what I'm going to say first. Maybe I should tell her I love her. Maybe that first. Man . . . come to think of it, I don't think I've ever told her that. That's incredible. All this time, and I don't think I've ever said it. You'd think I'd remember if I did, right? And I don't, so I must not have. Maybe I should say that first.

(Small pause.)

My mother always told me something. She always said, "You know, the way you treat your mother, that's the way you're going to treat your girlfriends—and when the time comes, it's the way you'll treat your wife." I told her, "Get out." I thought she was just try'na get me to stop picking my toes at the dinner table, you know? Or leaving my dirty underwear under the bed. I always thought she was crazy. Well, I haven't had a date in a while. Wait . . . wait a minute, now this isn't really a *date*, you know what I mean? It's not really . . . like a formal thing. Okay, I do have flowers. Come to think of it, I've never given her flowers. That blows me out. Never. You'd think I'd remember if I did, right. And I don't, so I must not have. Maybe I should just give her the flowers first. Anyway, what I'm saying is, it's not a "date" date, it's just that I asked her if I could take her somewhere nice. She deserves it. That's all there is to it. *(A beat.)* I don't think I've ever taken her anywhere nice. I'd probably remember if I did, right? And I don't. So I must not have.

(Pause.)

We're gonna be late. I wonder if she's ready. Maybe I should tell her we need to jet. *(Calling.)* Hey! Would you hurry it up! *(Smacks his head.)* Oh, great. Now that was smart. Mom was right. I have no idea how to treat a lady. None. Here I am screaming at her like my wrestling coach. *(Mocking himself.)* "Hey, hustle it up, wimp!" You know, the last date I had, oh, back in the last ice age, I think, we went to McDonald's before the concert, right? We order and sit down. She's the one that gets up to get the napkins and the straws. We eat. I get up to go. She's the one that cleans off the table and dumps the stuff in the trash can. Hey, Mom always did it, right? So we get to the concert, I buy the popcorn with double butter on it. I find out later she doesn't like butter. But Bozobrain here didn't even bother to ask. Well, dude, *I* wanted butter, right? Right. When I called to ask her out again, she tells me she's in training for the 1996 Olympics and she'll be busy every night and weekend for the next five years.

(Pause.)

My mom was right. Oh, don't look at me like that. Come on, she's not *always* right. *(A beat.)* But she's got a batting average that'd put her in the major leagues, I can tell you that. Dad . . . now Dad's still on the farm team, but Mom, she's a slugger. She hits 'em right out of the park. Like the time in the third grade when I told her Marion Schmidt hated my guts because she was always throwing junk at the back of my head during class, and my mom said, "No, she's got a crush on you." Boy was she right. I couldn't shake Marion till junior high.

(Pause. He looks at his watch.)

Well, you better believe I'm listening to her now. When she tells me how to treat someone, well, I sit up and take notes. She's already taught me more than I can even tell you. You know, about how to treat people. *(A beat.)* I just wish I didn't learn it by treating her so bad sometimes. *(Another beat. He smiles.)* I'll tell you something, but you gotta keep your gums zipped about it, got it? *(Leans in.)* I only hope that I can make as good a choice as my dad did. Okay, it's out. Remember, I'm trusting you.

(A deep breath.)

Well, I think we'd better get going. Lemme see . . . *(Pulls out a list and checks it.)* . . . She said I should . . . and make sure I . . . and don't tell her to "Look over there" and then steal her food. Okay.

(Folds the list and puts it away.)

I'm a little nervous about tonight. I'm not sure what to do yet. She means a lot to me, and I want her to know it. Okay, first the flowers, then, "I love you." Okay, okay. Here goes.

(He walks to the door.)

Hey, Mom? Are you ready?

(Blackout.)

Father Knows Better

A Monologue for Father's Day
Based on the Story of Jairus

Cast

FATHER: a man in his 30s to 50s
GIRL: his daughter, a girl about 11

Scene

A kitchen

Props

Chair
Tennis shoes
Shoelaces
Mitt
Baseball

Costume

Modern casual. GIRL is dressed in a Little League outfit.

Running Time

4 minutes

Production Notes

"Father Knows Better" is based on the story of Jairus who bucked his social status to come to Jesus and ask for healing for his dying daughter.

In this contemporary version, Father talks about how the loss of his control in the face of his daughter's sickness forced him to turn her over to Jesus. He quickly learns that part of the process of a child growing up is a father learning to turn her over. But to whom? In this sketch, Father learns the "whom" is Jesus.

This is a monologue that doesn't need to be rushed. There are several times when Father will need to get his emotions in check. Trying not to cry is often more effective than tears.

Time the lacing of the shoes to end up with the close of the monologue.

(Lights. A kitchen. FATHER *is dressed in jeans, T-shirt, and a baseball cap. A bat and a mitt lay beside him on the floor. He's putting new laces in his tennis shoes.)*

FATHER: I don't know about you, but I *always* know when my little girl is faking sick. *(Laughs.)* All I have to say is, "Come here, let me smell your breath." That's the trick, you see? They can groan, get themselves all flushed, figure out ways to get all clammy. Sometimes kissing the forehead to detect a fever? Even that can fool you. But not the breath. Sick breath always has that smell. It's . . . well, maybe it's a sour smell or something. All I can say is—you just know it when you smell it. So, I can always tell when she's faking it. *(Pause.)* This time she was not faking it.

(He wets down a lace end and gets it through the eyelet.)

There's always anxiety whenever your kid gets sick. You *know* it's just a flu bug or a cold or something. But whatever it is, you know you can't do a thing about it. Oh, you can treat her like an opera star, prop her up, buy her ice cream, give her medicine and 7-Up or whatever. But you always know you're treating the symptoms, right? You can't do a blessed thing about the cause. *That* she has to fight out all by herself. So. Big, strong, know-it-all-daddy has to give up all his power to this . . . thing, whatever it is. He has no control. No way to protect. And you *know* how much daddies love to control and protect. Even if they're still not very good at figuring out when and where to do it.

(Wets down another lace and threads it. He's gotten the laces crossed the wrong way. He sighs and firmly pulls the lace out and starts again.)

It wasn't a school day. That was my first clue. "Daddy, my skin hurts," she said from the kitchen. "Did you bruise yourself, honey?" "No, I mean all my skin. All over." So, I went over to the table where she was sitting and I kissed her forehead. It was pretty hot. "Let me smell your breath," I said. It seemed like she barely had the strength to get out some air. But it was, you know, that smell. I knew she was sick. "Honey, finish your breakfast and then go back to bed." And I went back into the other room for a few minutes. I walked back in just in time to catch her from toppling headfirst to the floor. She'd passed out. Sitting right there. I swept her into the bedroom like a lightning bolt. My stomach was balled up into a tight, little fist. I set her down and felt her forehead. Hot as a red coal now. "Honey, I'm going to call the doctor, okay? Honey?" She didn't open her eyes. She didn't open them again. Couldn't open them.

(Long pause. He gets his emotions under control.)

You know, daddies have to stand back an awful lot with their little children. You have to let go of the hands when it's time for them to slap their little feet across the kitchen floor all by themselves. Or when they march off to school, or off to their first job. You have to turn them over. Turn them over. That's where I always got stuck. I always knew I had to turn my little girl over. But to what? To whom? I never could figure that one out. Who knew her better than *me?* What she was afraid of, what areas she didn't think so clearly, what places she was ignorant. Eleven years I was dreading this, and now I had no choice. There was absolutely nothing I could do. I couldn't kiss away the sickness. I couldn't wipe it away from her cheek. It was ripping her right out of my hands. *(A beat.)* That's when I decided to turn her over to Jesus.

(Small pause. He sets one laced shoe aside.)

It surprised me when His name first popped in my head. It wasn't a name I thought of often. Hardly at all. *(Taps his forehead.)* But when I heard it up here, it ran through my whole body like warm water. I said it out loud. "I'll go to Jesus." And so I did. Now, I have to be honest, it's not easy for someone like me to go to Jesus. It's like admitting defeat for someone who knows how to handle anything. I even remember what I said to Him. I haven't talked to Jesus much in my life, so it's not hard to remember them. I went right to Him and fell on my knees before Him and I said, "Jesus, my little daughter is dying. If You would just put Your hands on her I know she'll be healed and live." And He heard me. I know He did. He said to me, "Don't be afraid, just believe." Well, I was about to be very afraid. And I was going to need a lot of belief. Because while I was with Him, I found out that my little girl had died.

(Pause.)

What do you do then? I felt like I had turned her over and lost her. But I was willing to do whatever it took to get her back. So I invited Jesus into her bedroom. I took Him right in there with me. I showed her pale, still little body to Him. He wasn't upset. He went right to her and took her hand. "Little girl, wake up." And she sat up. By the time she looked at me, the color had already rushed back into her face. I couldn't believe what I was seeing. I turned her over to Him, and He gave her life. His life. I'll tell you one thing, she wasn't the only one who woke up in that tiny bedroom that day. There was another pair of eyes opened, and they belonged to—

GIRL *(off)*: Daddy!

(GIRL comes in, dressed in a Little League outfit and carrying a mitt. She looks eager and impatient.)

Are we gonna practice or what?

120

FATHER: Yeah, we're gonna practice. I just needed to tie things up here a little.

(Turns to the audience.)

Needless to say, I turn her over a lot now. When she's sick. *(Smiles.)* And when she's faking.

(He stands.)

It's the best thing a daddy can do for his little girl. Sometimes it's the only thing.

(She tosses him the ball, and they head off as the lights go to:

(Blackout.)

Independence

A Monologue for the Fourth of July

Cast

CHUCK: a man in his 30s to 60s

Scene

A backyard

Props

Barbecue
Cooking utensils
Tofu hot dog
Veggie or tofu hamburger

Costumes

A barbecuin' getup—stained apron and baseball cap

Running Time

3 minutes

Production Notes

Now don't get Chuck wrong. He loves his country. And he loves the Fourth of July. He just never knew what Independence Day meant until he met Jesus Christ.

"Independence" is a short monologue about how Chuck discovered that the cross at Calvary is truly his Statue of Liberty.

Chuck is a simple, burger-and-beans kind of guy. But he's not a yahoo. So steer away from overcharacterization in that direction. His observations on contemporary life are more out of amusement than any deep betrayal at how the world has changed.

If you can't find tofu products, you haven't looked hard enough.

Please don't light the barbecue onstage.

(In the darkness, fireworks and a John Philip Souza march. Lights. A backyard. CHUCK, *dressed in a sauce-stained, red-white-and-blue apron and a baseball cap, is tending to the meats on the barbecue. He whistles along with the march for a moment. He then leans into the barbecue, disappearing behind the hood for a moment.)*

CHUCK: YOW! *(He pops up, blowing on his finger.)* You buy all these sophisticated utensils and you still think you can just push a hot dog over with your finger and not get burned. Whatta Bozo, I tell ya.

(Fans the barbecue a moment.)

You know, the look of the grill sure has changed in the last few years. All different. Used to be just burgers and dogs on the old barbie for the big Fourth'a July picnic. Now all you see is chicken. And not just chicken, no . . . it's *skinned* chicken now. You know, so there's less cholesterol. You can't get 'em all crispy anymore. The kids used to love that. And look at this . . . this is great. *(Holds up a wiener on a fork.)* A tofu hotdog. Can you believe it? It's my wife's. Yeah, that wiggly white stuff all colored with something to make it look like an Oscar Mayer. Is that un-American or what? Same with this. My sister Carla. *(Holds up a patty on a metal spatula.)* A veggie burger. Isn't that disgusting? It's madea' soy products, she told me, and vegetables and rice. And they shape it like this. All you do is slap some BBQ sauce on it, throw it on a paper plate, and you look just like everybody else.

(He laughs. Puts the hamburger back. Small pause.)

These days sure aren't like the Fourth'a Julys I remember. You know, you can't even set off fireworks anymore. All you can do is watch 'em. Don't get me wrong, they put on some great shows. In a lot of ways, it sure beats sitting there like an idiot waiting for that stupid rainbow snake to sizzle out. Remember those? Or watching one of those idiotic paper log cabins burn to the ground.

(Closes the hood of the barbecue.)

I'd have to say Independence Day has changed for me too. Fourth'a July just isn't what it used to be, that's for sure. That's because . . . well, I don't mean to sound sentimental and all, but for the first time in my life, I know what independence means. See, with the Fourth'a July, we kinda celebrate the . . . fruits of independence, right? I mean, we're born into freedom here already. Now, I know you're gonna say we have to keep fighting for it, but what I'm saying is in the U.S.A. we're born free and it's *after* we find ourselves in prison, isn't it?

(Sighs.)

I'm getting all tongue-tied. Let's cut to it, okay? Almost a year ago, I discovered someone named Jesus Christ. It was the day after last Fourth, as a matter'a fact. I just sorta . . . I don't know . . . put up the white flag, you know? "I surrender!" I just suddenly realized I was standin' on enemy turf, and I threw down my weapons and beat feet to the other side. Now, I didn't see any fireworks, no rocket's red glare, but I could never feel freedom any stronger singing "Oh, Say, Can You See?" I'll tell you that. And things've been changing slowly. I'm still a prisoner of war to some things. But, you know, once you've tasted independence, you can spot a ball and chain a mile away. And you can't wait to cut it loose.

(Small pause.)

In a lot of ways, I am so grateful for this country. I'll be the first to tell you I love the idea of the Grand Old Lady standing in the harbor, holding up that torch of freedom and all. Sometimes, when I see pictures of her with all the lights on and fireworks exploding behind, I get a lump in my throat and chills down my arms. But I'll tell you something: the Statue of Liberty is not Calvary. Two hunks of wood nailed together may not be a work of art, but it's priceless. It's not the symbol of one country. It's the symbol of a whole Kingdom. Like I said, it hasn't always been like this for me, but this Fourth I can tell you the Cross is where I got my liberty. That's where I finally got my freedom. There was a revolution fought in my honor, and the enemy lost. And now I have a declaration of independence that beats 'em all. It starts like this . . . "For God so loved the world . . ."

(Pause. CHUCK *looks off.)*

Hey, they're almost done, okay! Well, you got the potato salad ready? Yeah, I didn't think so. Okay, okay. I'll be right in. *(To the audience.)* I just have one question for all of you. *(He lifts the hood of the barbecue.)* Any of you got the faintest idea how to tell when tofu is done?

(Blackout.)

Saying Grace

A Sketch for Thanksgiving

Cast

MOM: a woman in her 30s to 50s
DAD: a man in his 30s to 50s
DAUGHTER: a teenager (can be played as SON)
JESUS: whatever age or gender

Scene

A dining room

Props

Table
Chairs
Walkman
Dishware
Thanksgiving decorations

Costume

Modern

Running Time

5 minutes

Production Notes

It all started when Mom invited Jesus to be with them at their Thanksgiving meal—and He showed up.

What follows is a change in one family's behavior as Jesus stops mouths from saying things that should not be said, and bends hands toward doing things that should be done.

"Saying Grace" is all about the control of Christ as we turn what we say and what we do over to Him. What happens over the Thanksgiving turkey in this house is nothing short of reconciliation.

Jesus needs to be seated where He can be seen by the audience. Remember, the actors cannot see Him, so no betrayal of His presence must show on their faces or in their actions. And when Jesus does effect change by putting a hand to a plate, it needs to look like the actor's action, not some ghostly presence floating things through the air.

(Lights. MOM and DAD are sitting at the Thanksgiving table. The table is set for four. MOTHER grins. Sighs a sigh of satisfaction. DAD looks like he could melt the Jell-O salad with one glance.)

DAD: Is she eating with us or not?

MOM: She said she'd be right down. Just give her a minute.

DAD: Look, I didn't eat any breakfast waiting for this meal. I'm ready to chow.

MOM: Honey, just another— (Almost singing it.) Oh, there she is!

(DAUGHTER strides in listening to her Walkman. She starts to sit.)

DAD: Oh, no, young lady! You take those off.

DAUGHTER (can't hear): What?

> (DAD reaches over and clicks off the tape. DAUGHTER pulls off the headphones. Sullenly:)
> What did you do that for?

DAD: I told you I don't want you listening to your Workman—

DAUGHTER: —Walkman.

DAD: —whatever—at the table. Especially at Thanksgiving. Now, siddown, you're upsetting your mother.

MOM (cheery): Oh, I'm fine!

DAUGHTER (pointing to the other place setting): Who's that for?!

MOM: Oh, a guest.

DAUGHTER: Mom! I thought you said it was just going to be us for Thanksgiving! I'm dressed like a slug! Who's coming? Is it Uncle Pookey! You said Uncle Pookey was going to go to—

MOM: It's not for Uncle Pookey, honey. (A beat.) It's for Jesus.

DAUGHTER: Say what?

DAD: She said it was for Jesus, all right? Now siddown, young lady, your mother's getting furious with you.

MOM: Oh, I'm fine!

DAUGHTER (smiling, sitting): I get it. This is one of Mom's cute holiday things. Like when she tried to make us sing "Silent Night" holding candles around the Christmas tree last year, or read that Easter poetry she wrote.

DAD: Never you mind that. If your mother wants to invite Jesus to Thanksgiving, He's certainly welcome. Okay, let's eat. (Forks turkey onto DAUGHTER's plate.)

DAUGHTER (very upset): What are you doing?

DAD: I'm dishing you some turkey.

DAUGHTER: I'm a vegetarian, Dad. I don't eat meat.

DAD: You're a what?

DAUGHTER: I told Mom last week. Mom, I told you last—

MOM: Yes, yes, you did, honey. I'm sorry, I forgot. How about some potato salad—there's only potato, onion, mayonnaise, and—

DAUGHTER/MOM: Bacon.

MOM: Oh, that's right. How about some stuffing and gravy—

DAUGHTER (whining): Lard. In the gravy.

MOM: Oh, that's right. How about a—

DAD: Roll! (Slaps a bun on DAUGHTER's plate.) A roll. There's plenty of those. (Smiles.) Fine. Now that we've got that settled. Let's say some grace, shall we? I think I'd like you to say grace, young lady. Maybe it'll help with the attitude, huh?

DAUGHTER: I'm not going to thank God for a dead bird—

DAD: I said I want you to say grace! Your mom's gonna start screaming in a minute!

DAUGHTER: Why don't we just ask Jesus to say it; He's sitting right over there—

MOM (bowing her head): Lord, we come to You in gratitude on this Thanksgiving Day.

(DAD and DAUGHTER bow their heads, a bit ashamed.)

We ask You to bless this food to our bodies. Make us ever mindful of the needs of others. We ask, Jesus, that You be present with us during this meal.

(As MOM *says this,* JESUS *comes in and sits in the open chair.)*

We invite You to be with us as we eat and as we speak. In Jesus' name. Amen.

DAD/DAUGHTER: Amen.

MOM *(cheery):* There! We're all together, aren't we?

DAUGHTER: Yeah, we look like a Kodak moment.

DAD: Let's hit the trough!

(They eat for a moment. MOM *watches them.)*

DAD *(to* DAUGHTER*):* Pass me the yams over there, will you?

    (DAUGHTER *makes no move.)*

    Hello there? Young lady, I said pass me—!

MOM: Oh, I'll get it!

*(*MOM *reaches for the plate.* JESUS *stops her hand. He slides* DAUGHTER*'s hand to the plate. Before she knows it, she's handing the plate to* DAD.*)*

DAD *(taking it, surprised):* Ah . . . thanks.

DAUGHTER *(bewildered):* Sure.

*(*DAD *serves himself some yams. Starts to put the plate down.* JESUS *stops his hands, turns the plate toward* DAUGHTER.*)*

DAD: Ah . . . you want some yams?

DAUGHTER: Yeah. Sure.

(He dishes her some.)

DAD *(smugly):* So what is this vegetarian thing, anyway? Don't you think that's pretty— (JESUS *puts his hand on* DAD*'s mouth.)*

DAUGHTER: Want to watch what I'm eating. Be more healthy.

DAD (JESUS *releases him):* Oh. That makes sense.

DAUGHTER: Maybe you should watch what you eat more.

DAD: Oh, come on, I— (JESUS *stops him again. A beat. Releases him.)* I'll give that some thought.

*(*MOM *chokes in amazement.)*

128

DAD: You okay, honey?

MOM: Oh, I'm fine! *(Starts to stand.)* Oh, I forgot to bring in the corn! I'll just run into the kitchen—

(JESUS gently pushes her back in her seat and lifts DAUGHTER to her feet.)

DAUGHTER: I'll get it. *(She goes out.)*

(DAD starts shoveling food in, face bent over his plate. MOM watches him. JESUS stops DAD's hand and lifts his face up to see MOM. He looks at her.)

DAD: The food is great, honey. Turkey is perfect.

MOM: Oh . . . ah, thank you.

(DAUGHTER breezes in with the corn.)

DAUGHTER: Got it. *(She sits down, about to put the plate down. JESUS stops her hand, turns the plate toward MOM.)* You want some?

> *(MOM nods, openmouthed. Takes some spoonfuls. JESUS turns the plate toward DAD.)*
> Dad?

DAD: Sure, honey. *(Ladles corn onto his plate.)*

MOM: I hope you like everything. I was saying to myself just before we sat down that I didn't think this year's meal was going to be very—

(JESUS puts his hand to MOM's mouth. He slides her plate in front of her. Small pause. She starts to eat. They are all eating now. Contented. JESUS stands back and watches.)

MOM: Isn't this food just wonderful!

DAUGHTER: It's great. Thanks, Mom.

DAD: The best. You always make great Thanksgiving meals, sweetheart.

DAUGHTER: Yeah, too bad Uncle Pookey missed it.

(Suddenly all three look up at each other. They turn and look at the "empty" place. They smile. They go back to eating as the lights go to:

(Blackout.)

129

Home(less) for the Holidays

A Sketch for Thanksgiving

Cast

LORNA: a woman in her 30s to 40s
RALPH: her husband, a man in his 30s to 40s
KYLE: a teenage boy
DANA: a teenage girl

Scene

A church banquet hall

Props

Table
Thanksgiving decorations
Dishware
Aprons
Chef's hat

Costumes

Modern

Running Time

4 minutes

Production Notes

Lorna had decided that for this Thanksgiving, she was going to make a differ-ence in people's lives by volunteering to cook and serve the church Thanks-giving meal.

Her family, however, had other ideas.

"Home(less) for the Holidays" is a short glance at what happens when one family decides to serve Jesus one holiday by serving others—turkey, mashed potatoes, corn, and cranberry sauce.

The homeless in the sketch are all mimed, so the actors will need to practice "seeing" them as they pass by the buffet table.

(Lights. A church banquet hall. RALPH LOWRY and his children, DANA and KYLE LOWRY, are lined up in front of a long folding table covered with bowls, platters, pitchers, etc. Thanksgivingy tablecloth and decorations. The three are wearing aprons, holding serving utensils, and are standing at attention. They look miserable. LORNA LOWRY, also in an apron, is inspecting them.)

LORNA: Uniforms?

RALPH/DANA/KYLE (indicating their aprons): Check.

(RALPH quickly slips on his stained chef's hat.)

LORNA: Utensils?

RALPH/DANA/KYLE (holding out the utensils): Check.

LORNA: Smiles?

(They break into complaining: "No way!" "I'll serve, but I won't smile!" "Honey, you can't really expect us to—" "Nuh-uh! No smile from me!")

SMILES!!

(They all freeze with placid, forced grins.)

That's better. That ought to make everyone feel right at home. A real Thanksgiving smile!

KYLE: That's just where we should be. Home!

RALPH: I'm missing the football game, honey.

LORNA: You're taping it, Ralph.

RALPH: It's just not the same.

DANA: I can't believe you volunteered us to do this on Thanksgiving, Mom. I'm supposed to be sitting in front of a plate, not handing them out.

LORNA: All right, listen to me. They're all out there waiting for us to open the doors. I want everyone to just knock off the complaining. I'm sorry I told Pastor that we'd serve the Thanksgiving meal to the homeless. I thought it was something you'd all want to do. Did I misjudge you guys?

(Silence.)

You tell me, where do you think Jesus would be on Thanksgiving, huh?

(RALPH *starts to speak.*)

If you say laying on the front room floor, begging for a Maalox and watching the Turkey Bowl game, I'm gonna ladle your head.

RALPH: I was gonna say He'd be right here, doing what we're doing.

KYLE/DANA (*clapping*): Good answer, Dad! Good answer!

RALPH: Hey, I've been in a Sunday School a time or two in my day.

LORNA: I know you're giving up a lot. But this is really important to me. I just couldn't spend another Thanksgiving making more food than the Confederate Army could eat, stuffing it into warped Tupperware, and eating leftovers until I was so sick I'd swear off food till Christmas. I wanted my food to make a difference this year. I wanted my blessings to be a blessing to others. I didn't want to just say grace for another year; I wanted to show some of it. God's grace.

RALPH: I understand, honey.

KYLE/DANA: Sure, Mom.

(*Small pause.*)

RALPH: So, how long do you think this is gonna take?

LORNA: Get to your places. I'm going to open the door now.

DANA: Mom. I've been kinda scared all morning about this. I don't even know these people. Are they gonna come in here and rant and scream and say all kinds of weird stuff?

KYLE: They're gonna smell like—

LORNA: Then don't smell 'em. And Dana, if they rant, give them two helpings and let 'em pass. Don't be afraid, okay? They're people. You're just giving food to hungry people. (*Claps her hands.*) Okay! They're going to file past this table here. Dana, you're on mashed potatoes and corn. Kyle, you're on stuffing and cranberry sauce. Ralph, you're on turkey and gravy.

(*They get into position.*)

KYLE: I don't believe this. When Susan asked me if we were goin' to Grandpa's radical farm for Thanksgiving, I had to tell her I wasn't even going to *have* a Thanksgiving.

LORNA: Oh, you'll have a Thanksgiving, all right. One I'm sure you won't forget for a while.

DANA: Couldn't we eat some of this first. I'm *starving!*

(LORNA *throws open the "door." In mime, she greets people as they pass by.*)

LORNA: Good afternoon, Happy Thanksgiving! Welcome. Hello there. Happy Thanksgiving. Welcome. Right this way.

(RALPH, DANA, *and* KYLE *have their forced smiles on, dishing out food at arm's length. But a change starts happening. They begin to lean in. The smiles become real. They start to talk to the people passing by.*)

RALPH: Uh . . . sure, we *all* did the cooking!

KYLE: No, I'm a junior this year.

DANA: I know. I love Thanksgiving too.

RALPH (*about* KYLE): Yes, yes, he is a handsome boy, isn't he?

DANA: Oh, is that your little girl?

KYLE: I don't know, my mom made the stuffing.

DANA: Thank you. God bless you too.

RALPH: Oh, don't worry. We'll get something to eat later.

KYLE: Yeah, that's a great jacket you got there.

DANA: THREE DAYS?!

    (*All silence.* RALPH, KYLE, *and* LORNA *turn and look at* DANA.)

    Mom. This lady hasn't eaten for three days.

LORNA: She must be hungry.

DANA: You must be *starving.* (*A beat.*) Can I give you a little more?

(*They freeze. The lights go to:*

(*Blackout.*)

Blessing Dressing

A Short Monologue for Thanksgiving

Cast

JULIA KIDD: a woman of any age

Scene

A studio kitchen for a cooking show

Props

Table
Bowl of stuffing
Turkey (yes, a real one)

Costume

Modern

Running Time

2-3 minutes

Production Notes

"Blessing Dressing" is a humorous monologue that uses some interesting visual aids to talk about the nature of God's blessings in our lives.

The sketch is built around a cooking show and calls for a real store-bought turkey and actual stuffing. This is not a monologue for the squeamish. However, you can make a turkey out of a large, brown paper bag with cut paper legs.

Julia is written to be delivered fast. It's as if she only has a limited time for her program, and so tosses in her cooking advice right into the mix of her discussion about God. Let her character plow right on through. The humor is in the speed.

(In the darkness, TV program music. Lights. A studio kitchen. JULIA, *standing at the kitchen table and wearing an apron, ready to stuff a turkey.)*

JULIA: Good morning and welcome to "The Gospel Gourmet." I'm Julia Kidd. I know what you're thinking. Thanksgiving will soon rear its gobbling, sage-and-parsley sprinkled little head, and I dedicate this show to those of us who sometimes have a little trouble with the thanks part of Thanksgiving.

(Pats the turkey.)

Let's start at the bottom, shall we? This little fellow, who so bravely agreed to be on our show this morning, represents us. Well, all right, maybe this looks like *some* of us long about May when we haven't seen the sun since October, hmmmm?

(Begins pushing handfuls of stuffing in to the bird.)

The stuffing I have here represents all the blessings of God. We call it Julia's Blessing Dressing. By the way, this is lovely chestnut stuffing, which I whipped up just before you joined me, that's how easy it is. You'll need chestnuts—always use fresh not canned because you're worth it—butter, chicken stock, celery, onions, apricots, sage, parsley, and eggs. A lovely holiday stuffing that takes about a half hour. Anyway, as I said, this stuffing is the blessings of God. And see where they are going? Right inside the bird. In fact, filling up the bird, as it were. Now, the bird has two ways of looking at this sudden inrush of wonderful blessing, doesn't he? Either he can believe that *he* is filling himself up with this lovely stuffing that will be the hit of any Thanksgiving meal—and you can trust me on that—or he can believe that he has nothing to do with it, doesn't deserve it, and the dressing is being prepared and placed inside him by someone else. Let's test out both theories.

(JULIA *pushes the stuffing bowl toward the bird.)*

Come on, Henry—we've taken to calling him Henry around the studio—fill yourself up with Blessing Dressing! By the way, this delightful stuffing recipe makes about 12 to 14 cups and can fill a 14-pound turkey. As you can see, our poultry pal has made no moves toward the bowl. You might say, "Of course, Julia, he has made no moves toward the bowl because the bird is dead." Well, I ask you, are we any better off if we turn away from the blessings of God? I have used Henry specifically because I believe we are as unable to pull down the blessing of God with our own wings as Henry is.

(Begins stuffing the bird again.)

But God is gracious, and He fills us up with good things that make us aromatic and flavorful, not dull, tough, and dry. Especially if you don't overcook but roast at a constant, moderate oven of 325 degrees for four and one-half to five hours for a 12- to 16-pound turkey, do not add water, and baste only once or twice with fat or drippings in the pan.

(Wipes her hands. Smiles.)

So, this is Julia Kidd saying, if it's between thanking yourself for what you have and thanking God, don't be a goose, which we'll be talking about next week. I have a lovely Danish roast goose with tart apples and prunes that is to die for. Until then, make sure you say grace and save the beaters for me. Bye-bye.

(Blackout.)